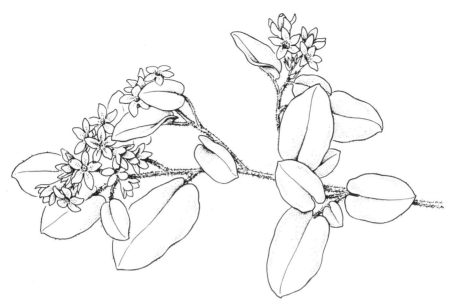

Suburban Wildflowers

An Introduction to the Common Wildflowers
of Your Back Yard and Local Park

Richard Headstrom

Illustrated by Bobbi Angell of the New York Botanical Garden

A Spectrum Book

Prentice-Hall, Inc., Englewood Cliffs, New Jersey 07632

Library of Congress Cataloging in Publication Data

Headstrom, Richard (date)
  Suburban wildflowers.

  (PHalarope books)
  "A Spectrum Book"
  1. Wild flowers—United States.   I. Title.
QK115.H386 1984   582.13'0973   84-3464
ISBN 0-13-859224-1
ISBN 0-13-859216-0 (pbk.)

This book is available at a special discount when ordered in bulk quantities. Contact Prentice-Hall, Inc., General Publishing Division, Special Sales, Englewood Cliffs, N.J. 07632.

·A SPECTRUM BOOK

ISBN 0-13-859224-1

ISBN 0-13-859216-0 {PBK.}

10 9 8 7 6 5 4 3 2 1

Printed in the United States of America

Editorial/production supervision: Joe O'Donnell Jr.
Book design: Joan Ann Jacobus
Cover design: Hal Siegel
Cover illustration: Bobbi Angell
Manufacturing buyer: Doreen Cavallo

Prentice-Hall International, Inc., *London*
Prentice-Hall of Australia Pty. Limited, *Sydney*
Prentice-Hall Canada Inc., *Toronto*
Prentice-Hall of India Private Limited, *New Delhi*
Prentice-Hall of Japan, Inc., *Tokyo*
Prentice-Hall of Southeast Asia Pte. Ltd., *Singapore*
Whitehall Books Limited, *Wellington, New Zealand*
Editora Prentice-Hall do Brasil Ltda., *Rio de Janeiro*

To My Sweetheart, Who Is Also My Wife

PHalarope Books

PHalarope books are designed specifically for the amateur naturalist. These volumes represent excellence in natural history publishing. Each book in the PHalarope series is based on a nature course or program at the college or adult education level or is sponsored by a museum or nature center. Each PHalarope book reflects the author's teaching ability as well as writing ability. Among the books:

The Amateur Naturalist's Handbook,
Vinson Brown

Botany in the Field: An Introduction to Plant Communities
for the Amateur Naturalist
Jane Scott

A Field Guide to the Familiar: Learning to Observe the Natural World
Gale Lawrence

The Plant Observer's Guidebook: A Field Botany Manual
for the Amateur Naturalist
Charles E. Roth

Suburban Wildlife: An Introduction to the Common Animals of Your
Back Yard and Local Park
Richard Headstrom

Trees: An Introduction to Trees and Forest Ecology
for the Amateur Naturalist
Lawrence C. Walker

Contents

Preface   *ix*

Introduction   *1*

Common Dandelion   *5*

Red Clover   *7*

Butter-and-Eggs   *9*

St. John's Wort   *11*

Queen Anne's Lace   *13*

Self-Heal   *15*

Chicory   *17*

Daisy, Ox-Eye   *19*

Jack-in-the-Pulpit   *21*

Blue Flag   *23*

Goldenrod   *25*

Bouncing Bet   *27*

Hepatica   *29*

Nightshade   *31*

Asters, New England Aster   *33*

Marsh Marigold   *35*

Skunk Cabbage   *37*

Trailing Arbutus   *39*

Dayflower   *41*

Forget-Me-Not   *43*

Tall Meadow Rue   *45*

Pearly Everlasting   *47*

Tall Bellflower   *49*

Yellow Meadow Lily   *51*

Four-Leaved Loosestrife   *53*

Oswego Tea   *55*

Wild Senna   *57*

Common Speedwell   *59*

Bluets   *61*

Frostweed   *63*

Tansy   *65*

Black-Eyed Susan   *67*

Common Meadow Buttercup   *69*

Showy Tick Trefoil   *71*

Common Milkweed   *73*

Mayapple   *75*

Yarrow   *77*

Night-Flowering Catchfly   *79*

Devil's Paintbrush   *81*

Moccasin Flower   *83*

Wood Anemone   *85*

Arrowhead   *87*

Turtlehead   *89*

Fringed Polygala   *91*

Spreading Dogbane   *93*

Bloodroot   *95*

Cow Vetch   *97*

Harebell   *99*

Wood Sorrel   *101*

Evening Primrose   *103*

Burdock   *105*

Jewelweed   *107*

Common Cinquefoil or Five-Finger   *109*

Wild Strawberry   *111*

Celandine   *113*

White Baneberry   *115*

Poison Hemlock   *117*
Pokeweed   *119*
Partridge Vine   *121*
Early Saxifrage   *123*
Wild Columbine   *125*
Indian Pipe   *127*
Blue Vervain   *129*
Common Mallow   *131*
Common Sunflower   *133*
Steeplebush   *136*
Cardinal Flower   *138*
Peppergrass   *140*
Water Lily   *141*
Meadowsweet   *143*
Boneset   *145*
Solomon's Seal   *147*
Wild Ginger   *149*
Mad-Dog Skullcap   *151*
Chickweed   *153*
Mullein   *155*
Virgin's Bower   *157*
Beggar-Ticks   *159*
Pickerel Weed   *161*
Thyme   *163*
Purple-Fringed Orchis   *165*
Gill-Over-the-Ground   *167*
Peppermint, Spearmint   *169*
Wild Indigo   *171*
Motherwort   *173*
Fireweed   *175*

Shepherd's Purse   *177*
White Clover   *179*
Yellow Rocket   *181*
Field Sorrel   *183*
Sweet Clover   *185*
Teasel   *187*
Indian Cucumber   *189*
Bladder Campion   *191*
Wintergreen   *193*
Canada Thistle   *195*
Blue-Eyed Grass   *197*
Lady's Thumb   *199*
Jamestown Weed   *201*
Butterfly Weed   *203*
Wood Betony   *205*
Dutchman's Breeches   *207*
Wild Geranium   *209*
Hedge Bindweed   *211*
Cattail   *213*
Downy False Foxglove   *215*
Blue Toadflax   *217*
Sundrops   *219*
Pussytoes   *221*
Common Violet and Violets   *223*
Glossary   *227*

Preface

Were we to envision a world without flowers in which to live—as if that were possible—we would find it a dreary place indeed. Flowers give color and beauty to the landscape, they enrich our lives with their aesthetic qualities, and more prosaically, they provide food for the table.

Many people accept flowers as natural features of the landscape and think no more about them—except that they may enjoy looking at them occasionally. Others grow flowers in the garden for the pleasure it gives them. Still others are interested in flowers in order to enrich their understanding and knowledge of the world around them and perhaps use identification manuals to accomplish this purpose. A very few pursue botany courses in college and become professional botanists.

This book is about the flowers that grow wild rather than those that are cultivated in the garden. It is about flowers that grow in the nearby fields, in the adjoining woods and along the roadsides, in swamps and marshes, along the banks of brooks and rivers, in ponds and lakes and along the seashore, and generally speaking, all within easy walking distance of where we live, whether in city, town, or village. It is not a field book, an identification manual, or a treatise on botany but a series of word pictures—vignettes if you will—of the various flowers that grow wild near at hand. It is about their virtues and vices, about the legends and folk tales that are associated with them, and about the uses to which many of them have been put. It is about the flowers that we might see throughout the year as we go back and forth to work, as we go about our work-a-day chores, as we go about the business of making a living, or as we go walking for a bit of exercise. And as we become better acquainted with them and begin to view them as friends, perhaps they might lighten our load in trying to survive in a highly competitive world by helping us to find a surcease in the contemplation of nature's wonders and handiwork.

Note: Although most wildflowers can be picked without depleting their numbers, there are a few that are fast disappearing from the scene and are on the verge of extinction. Such plants vary from state to state. What such flowers are can be found in *Endangered and Threatened Plants of the United States*, by Edward S. Ayensu and Robert A. DeFillipps. It is published by the Smithsonian Institution and the World Wildlife Fund. However, the secretary of state of each of the states should also be able to supply information for his or her own state.

Introduction

There are about 250,000 species of flowering plants on the earth and perhaps more; at least that many have been described and new species are added each year as the survey of the earth's vegetation continues and other materials are more critically examined. To that number of species should also be added the varieties, races, and strains, numbering in the thousands, that have been brought into being through man's efforts.

The group of flowering plants is the largest of all the groups into which the plant kingdom has been divided. These plants are the most varied and useful as well. This is because they provide food directly or indirectly for all other living organisms, though many of them may seem to be worthless weeds. They also provide hiding places for the creatures of the wild and furnish man with innumerable materials for his welfare and happiness.

The flowering plants show a great variety of forms; they may be simple minute disks that float on the water or of massive size such as some of the trees that grow to a height of three hundred feet and rival the higher animals in structural complexity. Some of them may live for only a few weeks, others for centuries. And they may be found in every sort of habitat: in the frozen wastes of the polar regions, in hot deserts, in the equatorial rain forests, on mountaintops, and on the seashore. Able to manufacture their own food, they are independent organisms, though some have become degenerate parasites or saprophytes and others have become carnivorous and feed on animals that they capture by means of ingenious traps.

The outstanding feature of a flowering plant is the flower. Most people know what a flower is, yet there are plants that produce flowers that most would not recognize as flowers. There are others that produce structures that would be taken for flowers but are not flowers in a botanical sense or in terms of the economy of the plant.

To define a flower is not easy because a flower is too complex and variable in structure and behavior to allow an easy definition. Put succinctly, a flower is a sex organ or combination of sex organs, or that part of the plant concerned with reproduction and the maintenance of the species. It is designed to produce male and female sex cells and is constructed so that a union of the two may take place; that is, the fertilization of the egg with the resulting production of fruits and seeds. And though flowers may vary greatly in detail, form, color, odor, size, and other things as well, they are all basically the same.

Thus the typical flower is borne on a stem called the *peduncle* and the enlarged end of this stem where the parts of the flower are attached is known as the *receptacle*. The parts or floral organs are the *sepals, petals, stamens,* and *pistils*. The outer or lower of these floral organs are the *sepals*. They are usually small, green, leaf-like structures, though they may be of almost any color, that enclose and protect the other floral organs in the bud before they are fully devel-

1

oped. Collectively they are known as the *calyx*. Brightly colored petals, usually conspicuous above and inside the sepals, are collectively known as the *corolla*. The number of petals is usually the same as the number of sepals, or it may be a multiple of that number. The purpose of the petals is to attract the insects whose visits are important to the reproductive function of the flowers. Flowers draw insects to them in several ways: with bright colors; with a sweet liquid called *nectar* that is desired by bees and other kinds of flower visiting insects and is secreted in glands called *nectaries;* and with odors from essential oils and other substances produced by special modified cells. Together the calyx and corolla constitute the floral envelop or *perianth*, important to the flower because it protects the delicate sex organs that lie within.

The male and female reproductive organs—the *stamens* and *pistils* respectively—are located inside and above the petals. There may be a few or many stamens in a flower. Each stamen consists of a slender stalk or filament surmounted at its apex by a single enlarged, often cylindrical or ovoid anther. The anther produces the pollen grains, which later lead to the formation of the male reproductive cells or *sperms.* The anthers are commonly yellow and each may produce a great many pollen grains—thousands, or even millions, in some flowers. These grains are liberated when slits or pores are formed in the anthers.

Situated in the center of the flower is the *pistil*, around which are located the *stamens, petals,* and *sepals.* It consists of three fairly distinct parts: an enlarged globular or bulbous base called the *ovary;* an elongated stalk or *style* that extends upward from the ovary; and at the top of the style, a slightly enlarged *stigma* upon which the pollen grains fall or to which they are brought by the wind or insects. The stigma is often expanded into a bulb or disk or cut into two, three, or more slender segments. It frequently is very rough or bristly and sometimes is covered with a sticky fluid so that the pollen grains will adhere. The ovary has a well developed cavity where the immature seeds or *ovules* are produced. The ovules, which are usually attached to the central axis of the ovary, are where the female reproductive cells, or *eggs*, are formed.

The ovary may be *simple* or *compound*. A *simple ovary* is composed of a single pistil or carpel, a *carpel* being a floral organ that bears and encloses ovules. A *compound ovary* is made up of two or more pistils or carpels firmly grown together. In *compound pistils* the styles are also usually united, sometimes to the top of the stigmas. A *simple pistil* or *carpel*—a *cell*—of a compound pistil may contain a single ovule or many ovules. The *pistil—ovary*—normally develops into a fruit and, in turn, each ovule becomes a seed contained in the fruit. The sepals and petals are usually referred to as *accessory organs*, the stamens and pistils as *essential organs*—the former because they are not directly concerned with the reproductive processes, whereas the latter are directly involved in the formation of seeds.

A flower with all the floral structures present is said to be *complete*. A flower lacking one or more is, of course, *incomplete*. Flowers that have both stamens and pistils are *perfect flowers*. Those that have only stamens or pistils are *imperfect.* Imperfect flowers with stamens are called *staminate flowers.* Imperfect flowers with pistils are described as *pistillate.* Where the stamens and pistils occur in separate flowers on the same plant, those plants are said to be *monoecious.* Where the two kinds of flowers occur on separate plants, those plants are said to be *dioecious.* A few species of flowering plants that produce their stamens and pistils in different flowers also produce perfect flowers. They are said to be *polygamous.* In species where the staminate and pistillate flowers occur on separate plants, the staminate plants cannot bear fruit.

In many flowers the sepals and petals are separate from each other. In other flowers the sepals appear to be united to produce a continuous girdle about the flower. The petals also appear united, basically forming a tubular or rotate corolla. The united part is the *tube* and the spreading part, or the lobed border, is the *limb.* Most flowers are beautifully symmetrical and are said to be *regular.* Others are unsymmetrical or lopsided because some of the petals on one side of the corolla are larger or differently shaped than the other parts of the flower. These are said to be *irregular.* Finally, the size of the flower, as represented by the spread of the open perianth, may vary from the almost microscopic in certain grasses and water plants to an enormous structure four or five feet in diameter and weighing as much as fifteen pounds. Such flowers occur in certain species of rafflesia. These are parasitic on the roots of grapes in the tropical forests of the Malay archipelago.

In some species of flowering plants the individual flowers are borne at the end of a long stalk or stem known as the *peduncle.* Such flowers are usually fairly conspicuous because of their relatively large size and bright colors. In most species however, the flowers—small or large, brilliantly colored or not—occur in groups or clusters and the stalks or stems of the individual flowers are known as *pedicels.* The main stem or the axis of the cluster is the *peduncle.* Flower clusters are generally known as *inflorescences.*

There are a number of different kinds of inflorescences—the *head, spike, catkin, spadix, raceme, corymb, umbel,* and *cyme* to name several. The *head* is a dense cluster of sessile or nearly sessile flowers on a short axis or *receptacle.* An example is the dandelion. A *spike* is an inflorescence in which the sessile flowers are arranged on a basically elongated common axis. An example is the plantain. Much like a spike, a *catkin* is really a spike-like inflorescence that bears only staminate or pistillate apetalous—*without petals*—flowers. A *spadix* is a spike with a fleshy axis bearing sessile flowers, for example, the Jack-in-the-pulpit. The spadix is commonly surrounded and partly enclosed by the *spathe,* which is a large bract or pair of bracts.

A *bract* is a modified leaf associated with a flower or an inflorescence. A *raceme* is a simple inflorescence in which the flowers, each with its own pedicel, are spaced along a common, more or less elongated axis. An example is the lily-of-the-valley. A *corymb* is a simple inflorescence in which the pedicels, growing along the peduncle, are of unequal length. Those of the lowest flowers are the longest and those of the upper flowers are the shortest. An *umbel*—the wild carrot is an example—is an inflorescence in which the stems of the flowers are approximately the same length and grow from the same point. A *cyme* is an inflorescence in which the apex ceases growth early and all its meristematic—*growing*—tissues are used up in the formation of the apical flower. Other flowers develop farther down the axis and the younger they are, the farther they are from the apex. An example is the forget-me-not.

Common Dandelion

A measure of success

It is human nature for us to view the commonplace with a certain degree of indifference and sometimes this indifference may border on the contemptuous. Few people speak well of the dandelion because it grows on our lawns and we regard it as a weed, a weed, according to the dictionary, being a wild plant that grows where it is not wanted. And so we dig it out or otherwise destroy it, considering it undesirable.

Were the dandelion a rare exotic everyone would extol its virtues. Yet it is those very virtues that make it a weed because the dandelion seems able to grow almost everywhere. That is one of the reasons why it is one of the most successful of plants—if success can be measured by the ability to meet the fierce competition for existence and survival, as the dandelion has been able to do. It is found throughout the civilized world and it more than holds its own wherever it occurs. As we look around we find it not only on our lawns but also in the fields, meadows, pastures, waste places, and along the roadsides. It is, in the words of James Russell Lowell:

> *Dear common flower that grows beside the way. . . .*
> *Which children pluck, and full of pride uphold.*

If we were to examine a dandelion plant dispassionately we would soon discover why it has been so successful. It has a large thick fleshy root that penetrates deeply into the ground, far below where heat and drought can affect it or where nibbling rabbits, moles, and grubs can break through and feast. It has a hollow stem that can bend before the strongest winds without breaking for, as any engineer will tell you, a hollow tube is stronger than a solid one. It has a rosette of leaves that extends from the root out over the ground, providing a barrier to keep other plants from growing too close, and which is left untouched by grazing cattle and sheep because it secretes a bitter, milky juice. It also has a golden yellow flower that dances merrily in the wind and that is actually not a single flower but a number of minute florets—sometimes as many as three hundred—all cooperating to ensure cross-pollination from small bees, wasps, flies, and other insects. These come seeking the nectar secreted in each little tube and the abundant pollen. Both are greedily appreciated, especially in early spring. After flowering, the golden head is transformed into a globular white airy mass of tiny parachutes, each one a seed ready to sail away on the slightest breeze, to be carried perhaps untold distances before finding a resting place.

The word *dandelion* does not refer to a dandy lion as some might infer from the way it is pronounced. It is a corruption of the French *dent-de-lion*. This means *a lion's tooth*, the name being given to the plant because the leaves were supposed to resemble a lion's tooth. However there has been a difference of opinion as to which part of the plant is supposed to resemble a lion's tooth. The view has also been advanced that the name refers to the yellow flowers that have been likened to the golden teeth of the heraldic lion.

For years the young leaves have been highly prized as a spring green for use as a potherb and for salads. The dried root has been used as a substitute for coffee in various countries and at different times.

Red Clover

A classic tale

There is the classic tale of how, many years ago, the Australian farmers imported the red clover seed to grow a crop of red clover as fodder for their cattle. They had a bounteous crop the first year but failed to get any seed to plant the following year simply because they had neglected to import the bumblebee as well. Once they had taken care of this oversight all went beautifully.

Almost everyone is familiar with the red clover because it often appears on our lawns. We also find it in fields and meadows and along the roadside. Moreover, it is extensively cultivated as a hay and pasture crop. As is the case with the dandelion, what we commonly call the flower is actually a number of small individual flowers or florets. These are closely crowded together into a somewhat pyramidal globular cluster that ranges in color from crimson or magenta to paler tints of the same colors. Each floret contains an abundance of nectar which is of little value to the honeybees—among the most efficient of pollinators—since their tongues are too short to reach down into the nectar wells. The butterflies, with their long tongues, can reach the wells easily and often drain the nectaries without giving any service because they are not heavy enough to depress the protective structure that guards the pollen from unwanted pilferers. Only the burly bumblebees can do so and hence they are the red clover's chief, if not its only, benefactors. When they sip the nectar their heads and tongues become covered with pollen which they then transfer to other flowers and thus effect cross-fertilization.

I can recall that when I was a boy we children used to suck the florets for their nectar with almost rapturous delight. No wonder we often see numerous butterflies, among them the fritillaries and sulphurs, flying about clover fields. The caterpillars of the dusty wing and of several other species feed almost exclusively on the leaves.

The leaves of the red clover are actually leaflets, having at some time become divided into three parts. They are oval, dull bluish-green, and each is conspicuously marked by a whitish or yellow-green triangle. At evening the leaflets fold downward, the side ones like two hands clasped in prayer, the end one bowed over them. It has been said that the name clover probably originated from the Latin *clava*—club—because of a fancied resemblance between the three-pronged club of Hercules and the clover leaf. The clubs of our playing cards are probably an imitation of this same leaf.

The common expression *he's in clover,* meaning to be in luck, in prosperous circumstances, or in a good situation, is an allusion to cattle feeding in clover fields. At one time the peasants of Europe believed that to dream about the flower would prophesy not only a happy marriage but also long life and prosperity. The clover has been regarded for ages as a mystic plant. All sorts of good and bad luck were said to attend the finding of a variation of its leaves which had more than the usual number of leaflets. I recall how as children we used to look for a four-leaf clover, the finding of which was supposed to bring us good luck.

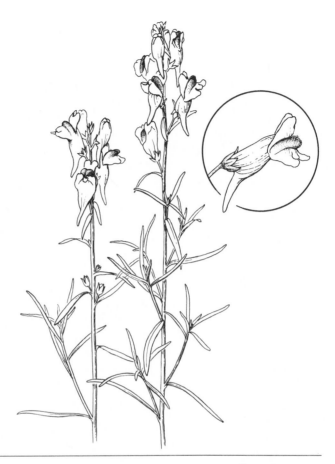

Butter-and-Eggs
A weed it is

Had it not selected to grow in waste places it could well have become a garden ornamental, for it is a beautiful plant with canary yellow and orange cornucopias and pale bluish-green leaves. But it is a weed and we find it growing in dry fields, pastures, city lots, and waste places along the roadside where it is so common that we invariably pass it by unless it should grow in masses. Then its beautiful and conspicuous blossoms may attract our attention but usually they do so only momentarily. We would consider it a pest if it did not display considerable discrimination in its choice of a place to grow, generally selecting useless pieces of ground and thus perhaps some day destined to inherit the earth.

We know it as the butter-and-eggs, which may seem a most unusual name for a wildflower. But it is most appropriate because its two colors perfectly match their namesakes. The flowers are about an inch long in terminal clusters and are two-lipped. The upper lip is two-lobed and the lower is three-lobed and pouch-shaped, tapering to the tip of a slender spur that contains the nectar. The opening to the flower is closed by an orange projection of the lip called a palate.

Guided by the orange palate pathfinder to where the curious flower opens, the burly velvety bumblebee comes seeking the nectar. It alights and its weight depresses the lower lip until a large enough opening is effected. Then in it goes, its long tongue reaching the nectar in the deep spur, and as it sips pollen is brushed off onto its body. When the bee has had its fill and backs out, the lower lip springs back after it and again closes the opening to the flower. Sometimes butterflies—such as the common sulphur and the Baltimore—may gain access to the nectar with their long, thin tongues but it is unlikely that they transport any pollen and thus aid in cross-fertilization. Beetles, which sometimes visit the flowers, occasionally obtain an entrance if nothing else. Even the ants are unable to reach the nectary when they succeed in entering the flower because a stockade of hairs bars their way. In stormy weather, when insects are not flying, the butter-and-eggs is able to fertilize itself. Indeed it has several qualities that enable it to successfully meet the stiff competition for survival. In addition to those we have already mentioned, it has a deep running rootstalk that is difficult to suppress and a taste and odor that cattle dislike. Thus in pastures it is unmolested and left to reproduce itself. The flowers have a cheesy smell that is reminiscent of the dairy. As a final thought, at one time farmers' wives mixed the juices of the leaves and roots with milk to make a poison with which to kill flies.

St. John's Wort

The talisman

There was a time when the peasants of Europe would gather the blossoms of the St. John's wort and hang them in their windows and on their doors on St. John's eve. They believed that by doing so they could avert the evil spirit and prevent the spirits of darkness from casting spells on their houses and their occupants. The name of the plant is said to have been derived from the superstition that the dew that fell on the plant the evening before St. John's day—June 24th—was effective in preventing diseases of the eyes. According to another superstition taken from Neltje Blanchan's *Nature's Garden*, if the plant were "gathered on a Friday, in the hour of Jupiter when he comes to his operation, so gathered or borne, or hung upon the neck, it mightily helps to drive away all phantastical spirits."

 And still another belief held that on St. John's eve the soul had the power to leave the body and visit the spot where it would finally be called from its earthly habitation: hence the all night vigils which were observed at this time.

The St. John's wort is also "The wonderful herb whose leaf will decide/If the comming year shall make me a bride." The maiden's fate is favorably forecast "by the healthy growth and blossoming of the plant that she accepted as typical of her future."

All sorts of virtues were ascribed to the plant: that it would reveal the presence of witches and expose their devilish practices, that it would cure those who were possessed of evil spirits, and that it would prevent destruction from lightning. Therefore the superstitious peasants permitted it to grow about their houses and barns in the belief that it would ward off witches and demons.

On a more practical note, both poets and physicians in early times extolled its healing properties. It was collected, dipped in oil, and made into a balm that was supposed to be a remedy for all kinds of wounds. One of its early names was *balm-of-the-warrior's wound*. It was also considered to be a cure for melancholy and hence was termed *funga daemonum*.

A perennial, brought to North America from Europe but a native of Asia, and a pernicious weed difficult to eradicate, the St. John's wort is a common wildflower found everywhere throughout our range. Its deep golden-yellow flowers bloom throughout the summer. The flowers later develop into ovoid brown capsules in showy clusters on a many branched stem that is one to two feet tall and bears small green leaves that are dotted brown. These signal its presence in fields, along roadsides, and in waste places. It is not a particularly attractive plant for it has a rather untidy unkempt look. This is because the seed capsules and the brown withered flowers remain among the bright yellow flowers during a long flowering season. The flowers do not secrete any nectar and so are visited only by pollen collectors that sometimes cross-fertilize them. However they are well adapted to pollinate themselves. When young, the plant contains juices that are so acrid and blistering that grazing animals leave it alone.

Queen Anne's Lace
The queen's embroidery

One of the loveliest of all our wildflowers is the exquisite Queen Anne's lace—more prosaically, the *wild carrot*—which we find throughout the summer decorating the fields, meadows, and roadsides with its lacy blossoms and fern-like leaves. Sometimes it even appears in our gardens—as it did last year in mine—where it need not take a back seat to any of the flowers that we normally grow. Indeed it would long ago have become a garden decoration if it were not so common and generally regarded as a weed. It seems to be human nature to view the common with a certain amount of contempt, as if of no account.

The Queen Anne's lace is one of the most successful flowers. Having proved its fitness in the fierce struggle for survival among the plants of the old world, it eventually made its way to our shores. Here it found conditions favorable for colonization in our vast uncultivated area and so began to crowd out the less aggressive occupants of our soil. What has made it so successful? As with other successful plants, its flower is designed to attract and utilize a great many insect visitors, in this case sixty or more different species—flies, beetles, wasps, bees, and butterflies. The nectar is secreted in open disks near one another where even insects with the shortest tongues can have access to the sugary liquid. Doubtless many of the insects are attracted to the flower by its peculiarly strong odor.

We must examine the lacy clusters with a hand lens or magnifying glass to appreciate their delicate structure and perfection of detail. The naked eye cannot do it. What appears to the casual observer to be a single cluster is actually a number of small clusters of white flowers that are disposed in a radiating pattern like a handmade piece of lace. In the center of the entire cluster there is a tiny purple floret that is not a part of any of the smaller clusters but is set upon its own isolated stalk. No one has yet been able to account for it. When the flowers have served their purpose the entire cluster dries and curls up to resemble a bird's nest. Hence the Queen Anne's lace is also known as the *bird's nest*.

Some years ago, by cultivation and selection over a period of years, roots as fleshy and as large as those of the cultivated carrot were obtained from the wiry roots of the wild carrot. Presumably these experiments were conducted to prove that the wild carrot is the progenitor of the garden species. However if the cultivation of the garden carrot is allowed to lapse for a few generations it reverts to the ancestral type, a species quite distinct from the wild carrot.

The garden carrot was well known to the ancients. For instance, Caius Plinius Secundus—Pliny—wrote that the finest specimens were brought to Rome from Candia. John Gerarde, the English herbalist of the sixteenth century, spoke of the plant and it is believed to have been introduced into Great Britain by the Dutch in 1558. John Parkinson, the English herbalist of the seventeenth century, wrote that the ladies wore carrot leaves in their hair in the place of feathers. As Mrs. William Starr Dana put it, "one can picture the dejected appearance of a ball-room belle at the close of an entertainment."

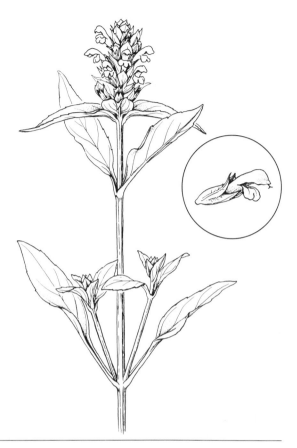

Self-Heal
The panacea

When we see it growing along the roadside it is frequently dusty, stunted, and bedraggled in appearance but when we find it afield and along the woodland border it is bright and sprightly and a rather cheery little plant.

I am writing of the wildflower which we know by the name of *self-heal*, though it has other names as well. One is *heal-all*, which may be more appropriate, as we shall see. It is a low growing perennial, and immigrant from Europe as many of our wildflowers are, generally with a single square stem, somewhat oblong leaves, and tubular two-lipped hooded flowers that are set closely together in a cluster that reminds us of the clover head. The flowers are tiny, purple, violet-blue, or sometimes white, and beautiful to look at when the plant is found growing under the most favorable of conditions.

It is a plant that adapts itself to circumstances: Sometimes its stem is erect or ascending, sometimes prostrate; sometimes it is not more than two inches tall and its flowers are barely visible among the grasses, at other times it may be as much as twelve inches tall and its flowers may be seen from a distance. It is a tireless bloomer with an unusually long flowering season: Hence the seeds are ripening and falling all summer. It is well attended by the bumblebee, assisted at times by the common sulphur butterfly. Is it any wonder, then, that we find it everywhere: in fields and along the woodland borders, in the roadsides and in waste places, and frequently on our lawns. And so we regard it as a weed and do not cultivate it as a garden ornamental—although at times we do use it for damp and shady places.

Several centuries ago the self-heal was used as a remedy for quinsy and its botanical name was *Brunella.* Doubtless this was derived from the German word *braüne*—quinsy. The Swedish botanist Carl Linnaeus changed this to *Prunella.* As Parkinson informed us in writing of the plant: "This is generally called prunella and brunella from the Germans who called it brunellan, because it cureth that disease which they call die bruen, common to soldiers in campe, but especially in garrison, which is an inflammation of the mouth, throat, and tongue." The old herbalists used the plant to cure—or at least to pretend to cure—every ailment that afflicted the people and to treat all sorts of wounds suffered by laborers and peasants. Hence it was given such names as *carpenter's herb, hook-heal, sicklewort, slough-heal,* and *brownswort.* The French also used the plant for similar purposes, as we learn from an old proverb of theirs: "No one wants a surgeon who keeps Prunelle."

Chicory
The substitute

In his poem "The Humble Bee," Emerson spoke of the succory as matching the sky:

> *Grass with green flag half-mast high*
> *Succory to match the sky.*

Succory is the *chicory*, a perennial wildflower, naturalized from Europe, that many of us know so well and that we find growing in fields, meadows, pastures, roadsides, and vacant city lots.

It is a stiff, branching plant with a deep taproot. It has a stem from one to three feet in height with small clasping leaves but with larger leaves from three to six inches longer emanating from the base and forming a rosette on the ground similar to that of the dandelion. The flowers are sessile and clustered—though sometimes they occur singly—from an inch to an inch and a half in diameter and of a beautiful blue color. It is because of their color that the plants are frequently called the *Blue-Sailors.* The flowers, which are also similar in form to those of the dandelion, though they consist of fewer, though more highly developed, florets, are occasionally white or pinkish. They open only in the sunshine, usually close at noon, and remain closed during cloudy or rainy weather. They are capable of self-fertilization but are usually cross-pollinated by the honey bee, the leaf-cutter bee, and various species of mining bees.

Because of its distinctive beauty the chicory would be a valuable addition to any garden if we did not regard it as a weed. Other peoples regard it, not as a weed, but as a source of food and in many places cultivate it for this purpose. As a matter of fact, the chicory has been used as a salad plant from time immemorial. We do not know whether the ancients cultivated it but we do know that they were aware of the wild plant and its uses as a vegetable. Virgil wrote, while in a practical mood, "And spreading succ'ry chokes the rising fields" and Horace wrote that its leaves formed part of his frugal fare. Pliny also mentioned that the Egyptians valued it as an important plant in their diet.

Because of its deep taproot it is likely that the name *succory* was derived from the Latin *succurrere,* which means to run under. But the word *chicory* is Arabic and was applied to the plant by the Arabian physicians, who were so influential in Europe following the Conquest that other countries also adopted variations of this name.

The sixteenth-century English herbalist, Gerarde, mentioned the plant in his writings but didn't say anything about it being cultivated. However, in 1682 John Ray, the English naturalist, wrote that it was grown in gardens.

For years the young leaves of the chicory have been gathered in the spring, boiled as a potherb, and served like spinach. They have also been forced and blanched in a dark place and sold as a salad known as *barbe de Capuchin.* The roots, too, are often boiled and served like carrots and parsnips but they have never become popular. They are also ground and roasted as a substitute for coffee or as an adulterant mixed with coffee, many people preferring the admixture because of its flavor and regarding it as a more wholesome beverage. It is also cheaper than pure coffee. In Europe chicory is a farm crop and millions of pounds are exported annually to the United States. So great is the demand for it that in spite of its inexpensiveness it is often adulterated with roasted wheat, rye, acorns, and carrots.

Daisy, Ox-Eye

A lover's lament

If we were to stroll along a country road in May we might suddenly see a whitened field in the distance and for the moment wonder if nature had been in one of its prankish moods and had sent a belated snowstorm that way. But of course, the seemingly snowy mantle that covered the field was simply innumerable daisies that had opened their golden centered blossoms to the sky, to delight the eye of the beauty lover and to strike dismay in the heart of the farmer. And as we approach nearer we hear music bubbling up "in a cascade of ecstasy from the throats of bobolinks that are nesting among the daisies."

The daisy—or *ox-eye daisy* to give it its complete name—is perhaps the most common plant of the field and wayside. It is a favorite with children and artists but not with farmers and it is often called the *farmer's curse* because it is harmful to pasture land and difficult to eradicate. Like many other of our wildflowers it is an immigrant from Europe, having been brought to our shores by the early colonists. One of its centers of distribution in America is said to have been Saratoga and the route of Burgoyne's army. His horses were fed upon fodder that came from central Germany. The daisy was mixed with it and its seeds germinated in the wake of his army.

In his *Fieldbook of American Wildflowers* F. Schuyler Mathews wrote that "the flower's form is the summum bonum of simplicity and decorative beauty." Like the dandelion, the daisy is not a single flower but a cluster of hundreds of tiny, tubular yellow florets—each a perfect flower, being both male and female—packed tightly together within a green cup and surrounded by white ray florets that are female only. The flower head surmounts an erect slender stem, one to three feet in height, which springs from a short thick rootstalk fringed with fibrous rootlets. The leaves are dark green and ornamentally lobed, with those at the base forming a tufted mat. The others are sessile and clasping. It is said that the leaves may be eaten as a salad and the flowers are often gathered for decoration because they last for a long time.

Look closely at a daisy and you will likely see the thrips—minute black insects—threading their way in and out of the tiny florets. They are curious insects with very short transparent wings, curiously shaped mouthparts, and feet ending in a sort of cup. Into this cup is fitted a delicate protrusible membranous lobe or *bladder* that is adhesive and that enables these insects to cling to smooth surfaces.

The daisy, or *ox-eye daisy*, is not a daisy at all but a chrysanthemum with an unusually long name for such a small flower: *Chrysanthemum leucanthemum*, which is from the Greek and means *golden flower*. The true daisy is the daisy of England—*Bellis perennis*—which was first called the *day's eye* because it closed at night and opened at dawn.

> *That well by reason men it call may*
> *The Daisie, or else the eye of the day*

as Chaucer wrote some six hundred years ago.

Most of the English poets—Shakespeare and Wordsworth included—have extolled the virtues of the English daisy, the "Wee, modest, crimson-tippit flower" of Burns. But few if any have written about the ox-eye daisy, which is also known in England as the *moon daisy* and in Scotland as the *dog daisy*.

I recall that as children we often used the flower in childish divination to establish the state of our love life in the manner of Marguerite in Goethe's *Faust*, who plucks the petals to the refrain:

> *He loves me, he loves me not, he loves me.*

Jack-in-the-Pulpit

A quaint little preacher

If we find ourselves in a damp woodland on a day in spring we are likely to see a quaint little preacher standing in his parti-colored pulpit, delivering a sermon to the elves and sprites of the woodlands in a language of their own—one as solemn as we might hear in our own places of worship. In the words of the poet:

> *Jack-in-the pulpit*
> *Preaches today*
> *Under the green trees*
> *Just over the way . . .*
> *Come hear, what his reverence Rises to say.*

The fanciful *Jack-in-the-pulpit*—also known more prosaically as the *Indian turnip*—is at home in moist woodlands and thickets where it grows to a height of between one and two and a half feet. It is not an unattractive plant, its two long-stemmed, three-parted green leaves overshadowing the hooded flower beneath them. The flower consists of a curving ridged hood, known as a *spathe,* which is merely a modified leaf and which is commonly called the pulpit. This envelopes an erect club, known as the *spadix,* which is merely a flower cluster called a *spike* and which is the *Jack.* The spadix is two to three inches long. The small, greenish-yellow flowers are clustered on the lower part of the spadix and are either male or female, though occasionally both male and female may occur on the same spadix. The curiously shaped spathe is somewhat variable in color—green and maroon or whitish-striped. In the open, where it is more or less exposed to sunlight, it is paler than when found in the deep woods where it is more commonly a dark purple.

As the flowers generally occur on different plants they must depend on the insects for cross-pollination. These are usually small species known as the fungus gnats, which have recently transformed from maggots in mushrooms or decaying logs. But sometimes they fail to perform their mission of transferring pollen because they become imprisoned in the narrow confines between the bases of the spadix and spathe. As we have just mentioned, occasionally both kinds of flowers occur on the same spadix but this is the exception rather than the rule. It suggests the possibility that the plant's dependence on insects for fertilization may be a recent development.

In time the spathe falls away revealing a cluster of globular, green, shining berries that eventually turn a brilliant scarlet and that are eaten by various forms of wildlife which distribute the seeds far from the parent plant. The Indians also used the boiled berries for food.

The Jack-in-the-pulpit is not only an interesting plant above the ground but it is an interesting one below the ground as well. It has a solid, flattened underground stem called a *corm* with a fringe of coarse rootlets encircling the upper portion. This is a veritable storehouse of food, so much so that the Indians used it as a food and hence the plant became known as the *Indian turnip* because of its shape. It is true the corm is very starchy but it is also possibly the most stinging burning object to be found in the woods. It is believed that the Indians removed the burning taste by boiling it—perhaps several times—then drying the corms, and finally grinding them into a meal which they baked into cakes or used as a gruel.

Blue Flag
The royal emblem

Perhaps many of us would not care to venture into a marsh or swamp or even to approach the wet margin of a pond. However, were we to cast caution to the winds and visit such a place in May we would be greeted by phalanxes of blue flags standing in array, their royal color giving beauty to what otherwise might be a scene of sombre aspect. In both form and color the blue flag is doubtless the most regal of all our wildflowers. It is regal in both meanings of the word for the youthful and pious crusader, Louis VII of France, chose it as the emblem of his house, though the species which he selected as his badge may have been white. At that time spelling doubtless left something to be desired and the *fleur-de-Louis*—flower of Louis—soon became corrupted into its recent form of *Fleur-de-lys*. As Ruskin wrote, this is the "flower of chivalry with a sword for its leaf and a lily for its heart." The blue flag is a democratic flower—in the marsh one

jostles the next—and yet it is one that is indeed "born to the purple." As Long-
fellow wrote:

> Born in the purple, born to joy and pleasance
> Thou dost not toil and spin,
> But makest glad and radiant with thy presence
> The meadow and the lin.

The blue flag—also known as the *blue iris*—is a handsome and decorative plant of our wetlands with a straight almost circular stem two to three feet
in height. It has erect sword-shaped light-green leaves, folded and in a compact
cluster at the base. And it has a flower two to three inches long that is divided
into six sections—the outer three are spreading and recurving, with one of them
bearded, and the inner three are erect—all united into a short tube. It is violet-
blue, variegated with tints of yellow or white, and purple veined. It was named
the *iris*, after the Greek for rainbow, by the ancients, who were always apprecia-
tive of the aesthetic.

To the amateur botanist the structure of the blue flag's flower is extremely puzzling because the various parts are so grown together and thus are
not easily distinguished. However, to the professional botanist the plant is of
special interest because of the manner in which the flower is so beautifully con-
trived to ensure cross-pollination by the insects and especially by the bees. At the
same time it is ingeniously guarded against self-fertilization. In short, there is no
likelihood of seed being set unless pollen is obtained from another flower. And
now we may well ask what the chances are of pollen being thus secured. First of
all the flower is unusually large and showy and, because of its size and shape, it is
sure to attract the attention of a passing bee. Second, the color is both conspicuous and one that has been found to be especially attractive to bees, blue and
purple flowers being more commonly sought by these insects. So when a bee
alights on the only convenient landing place, namely, one of the recurved divisions of the flower, it only needs to follow the purple veins and golden lines,
which it has found by experience to lead to the nectar, to arrive at the nectar
well, and there to sip its fill of the sugary fluid. And as it does so it becomes
powdered with pollen that it carries to another flower.

It is said that the common sulphur butterfly and one of the skipper butterflies also visit the blue flag but whether or not they benefit the plant is a moot
point.

The rootstalks of iris contain an acrid resinous substance, called *irisin*,
which causes a purging, burning, and congesting of the intestinal tract of animals if eaten in large quantities. However cases of poisoning are rare for animals
usually leave the rootstalks alone because of their acrid property. Incidentally,
some people may receive a severe dermatitis from handling the rootstalks or, for
that matter, any other part of the plant.

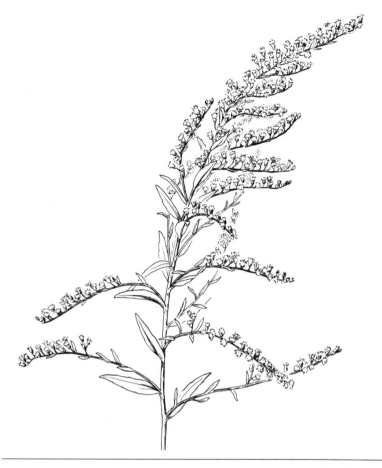

Goldenrod

They dress the fields in a cloth of gold

The first of our goldenrods appear in July and from then until September, when they dress the fields in a cloth of gold and sway by the roadside in every passing breeze, others follow:

> *Along the roadside*
> *Like the flowers of gold*
> *That tawny Incas*
> *For their gardens wrought*
> *Heavy with sunshine*
> *Droops the goldenrod.*

The goldenrods are coarse somewhat weedy plants, often branched or arching, with alternate usually toothed leaves and small yellow flower heads. These are very numerous in crowded or bushy, often elongated and plume-like clusters. Detach a flower stem and look at it with a magnifying glass or hand lens and you will be surprised at what you see—a row of tiny goblets.

The ease with which insects can collect both nectar and pollen from the goldenrods serves to make them popular restaurants. Bees, wasps, flies, and beetles swarm about them in immense numbers. It is said that no flower attracts as many insects as this popular blossom of the autumn landscape and I can well believe it. Among the more frequent visitors are the locust borer, a beautiful black beetle with numerous wavy yellow bands, and the blister beetle, a black beetle that is frequently found in such large numbers that the golden plumes appear as if sprinkled with soot. And later, when the brown plumes stand etched against the sky above the snow covered fields, sparrows, goldfinches, and juncos help to scatter the seeds as they satisfy their hunger on the down-curved stalks.

To the untrained eye the goldenrods may all look alike but many of the more common species have perceptible differences that serve to identify them. Thus the blue stemmed goldenrod, a woodland species, has a distinct bluish or purplish, plum-like bloom on the stem. The broad-leaved goldenrod, also a woodland species, may easily be recognized by its zigzag stem that grows waveringly, as if not sure what direction to take.

One of the easiest goldenrods to identify, especially when in flower, is the white goldenrod, or silverrod, because it is the only goldenrod with white flowers. It is common on dry barren ground. A species that grows in bogs and swamps, the bog goldenrod has a wand-like stem with leaves that gradually increase in size, the lowest being as much as nine inches long. The showy goldenrod is a handsome, stocky plant that grows in dry open woods and thickets. With a stem that rises from three to seven feet in height and golden flower heads that occur in dense somewhat pyramidal clusters, it is one of the more attractive of the group. And the rough stemmed goldenrod is well named, for it has an exceptionally hairy stem. It grows on wooded roadsides and on the margins of fields and is a perversely variable species.

Crush the dotted bright green leaves of the sweet goldenrod and you will readily recognize the plant by the pleasant anise scent it gives off. It is a goldenrod of dry fields and open woods with a simple slender stem crowned with a graceful panicle whose branches have the florets all on one side. This goldenrod is sometimes known as the Blue Mountain Tea because a beverage which is quite pleasing can be brewed from the leaves. But doubtless the most common of all the goldenrods is the Canada goldenrod. It is the familiar goldenrod of thickets, roadsides, and copse borders, where its large spreading densely-flowered plume-like panicle crowns a rough hairy stem that is sometimes as much as eight feet tall.

Bouncing Bet
The washerwoman

The reader may wonder if the author has temporarily taken leave of his senses or is in a playful mood, to head a vignette on a wildflower *The Washerwoman*. How could a plant possibly come to be so named? But that is its name—at least it is one of them—and how it came to get such a name we shall see presently.

Many of us are familiar with the plant commonly known as *bouncing Bet*, if not by name at least by sight, for it is common along roadsides, banks, and waste places. A native of Europe but long ago an escapee from colonial gardens, it is a stout strong growing perennial with a sparingly branched, smooth stem that reaches a height of three feet. It has ovate or broadly lance-shaped leaves and scallop tipped pink or white blossoms in a terminal cluster. The blossoms have an old-fashioned spicy odor, a single flower remotely resembling the flower of the pink.

Long ago a garden favorite—and still a favorite for the garden border—

it is a buxom and exuberant lass among the flowers. Its "feminine comeliness and bounce" suggested to John Burroughs a Yorkshire housemaid. Butterflies, which delight in bright colors, have little interest in the flowers but the night flying moths are able to see them in the darkness and are attracted by the fragrance, which becomes more pronounced after sunset.

Somewhere in the past, when the art of soap making was in its infancy or at least had not attained the excellence of today, someone discovered that a slippery sudsy solution could be made from the leaves by bruising them with water. Some housewife apparently made the further discovery that she could use the soapy solution to wash her woolens and silks. In time other housewives also made use of the plant for the same purpose and to be sure of having an available supply handy at all times they grew a patch of the plant in their gardens. So that the plant might have a name it gradually came to be known as *bouncing Bet*, which was a nickname for washerwomen. And as might be expected, the plant acquired other names with the passage of time: the *soapwort*—a name that is in common use today—*bruisewort, scourwort, Fuller's Herb, Old Maid's Pink, Sweet Betty,* and *Lady-by-the-Gate.*

The flowers have a five-toothed tubular calyx, ten stamens, and two styles. They bloom from July through September and develop into oblong conic capsules that contain dark slate or black seeds. These contain poisonous saponins—soap-like substances.

Hepatica

Of delicate beauty

If we are of an intrepid nature and venture into the woods during the month of March, when snow is still on the ground and chilling winds weave their way through the leafless branches, we might, if we are lucky, come upon an unexpected surprise. There we might find the exquisite and seemingly delicate hepatica blossoming among the snows. We are surprised because we normally associate flowers with the warmth of summer.

> Blue as the heaven it gazes at,
> Startling the loiterer in the naked groves
> With unexpected beauty;
> for the time
> Of Blossoms and green leaves is yet afar.

I can still recall the time when I first saw this flower some years ago, wrapped in fuzzy furs for protection against the wintry elements. With raptuous delight I stood and looked at it as if I could not believe my eyes at what I saw. For the hepatica is the first of the wildings to appear, if we exempt the skunk cabbage, and it is usually only by chance that we find it blooming beneath the decaying leaves of the woodland floor, in some hidden nook, or beneath the lingering snows that have withstood the warm rays of the spring sun.

"There are many things left for May," wrote John Burroughs, "but nothing fairer, if as fair, as the first flower, the hepatica. I find I have never admired this little firstling half enough. When at the maturity of its charms, it is certainly the gem of the woods."

The hepatica is a low growing plant with three-lobed olive-green leaves that persist throughout the winter, the newer leaves developing after the flowers. The stems and flower stems are extremely hairy and the latter bear solitary pinkish, purplish, lavender, blue, or white flowers. It is a capricious plant for it varies in fragrance as well as in color. Sometimes it is the purple flowers that are sweet scented, sometimes the white, sometimes the pink. Only by sniffing them can we find those that are fragrant. The odor is faint and reminiscent of violets. The flowers are one-half to one inch wide with between five and nine sepals. They lack petals, have many stamens and several pistils, and have three green sepal-like oval to elliptic bracts surrounding the flower. They bloom from March to June.

Hepatica is the name of the genus to which it belongs and it is from the Greek for *liver*. The name was given to it because of the fancied resemblance between the shape of the liver and the shape of the leaves; hence it is also known as the *liverleaf* and *liverwort*. For this reason the early herbalists believed that the plant was an effective remedy for all sorts of liver ailments. But not so the American Indians, who used the plant to cure vertigo, cross-eyes, and coughs.

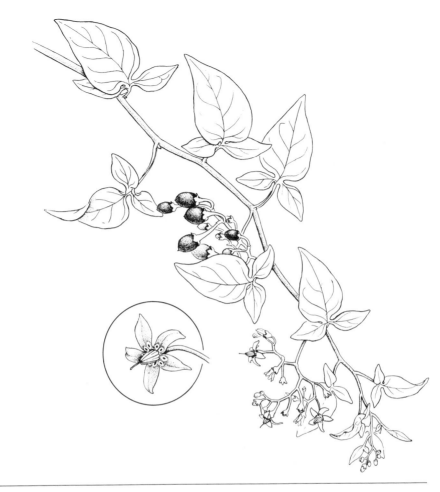

Nightshade
Lanterns in the thicket

On almost any day in late summer or early autumn, should we be walking along a shady road, our eye will most likely be caught by the shining berries of the nightshade. They gleam in the tangled thicket like little red lanterns at a time when the unpretending vine has weaved its way through the rank vegetation of midsummer and has become a joy to behold.

The nightshade, like many of our other wildflowers, an importation from Europe and common throughout our range, is found not only along roadsides but also along fence rows and the banks of streams, in waste places and in ditches, and in our yards as well. It is a climbing, scrambling, almost shrub-like plant with variable dark green leaves. The leaves are ovate to triangular in outline, some are lobed, others are formed of three leaflets. The plant also has small pendant wheel-shaped bluish or purple blossoms with yellow conic centers. The blossoms gradually turn from green to yellow and then to orange and scarlet berries.

The nightshade is a most decorative and useful plant, for migrating birds apparently find the berries pleasing to their taste. The hard indigestible seeds pass through them unaltered and are voided many miles away—a nice refinement to ensure wide distribution of the plant. The wilted leaves of the plant are poisonous and cattle, horses, and sheep have been poisoned by eating them. The berries are poisonous also. Children find them attractive and so they should be warned against eating them.

Regarding them Thoreau wrote:

> *The berries are another kind which grow in drooping clusters. I do not know any clusters more graceful and beautiful than these drooping cymes of scented or translucent, cherry-colored elliptical berries. They hang more gracefully over the river's brim than any pendant in a lady's ear. Yet they are considered poisonous; not to look at surely. . . . But why should they not be poisonous? Would it not be bad taste to eat these berries which are ready to feed another sense?*

An unusual feature of the nightshade is that any one vine may show all stages of coloring, from violet flowers to green and ripe fruit. At one time it was used in England to ward off witches and evil spirits. Sometimes it is also known as the *bittersweet* because some portions of the plant first taste bitter, then sweet.

Asters, New England Aster

Stars on the landscape

Although some asters may blossom in July and others is August, these are essentially autumn flowers. That is when they flood the landscape with royal color. Botanists have named some 250 species and of this number about 120 are native to North America.

The asters are usually bushy plants with alternate leaves and flower heads that may be solitary or in clusters. From a distance they appear as central yellow disks surrounded with an outer ring of what appear to be petals—floral leaves—that is variously colored in white or in tints of blue, violet, or purple. The central disk is composed of many erect tubular blossoms that are perfect—both male and female—and that are yellow at first but change with age to purple or brown. The outer ring of what appear to be petals are elongated and strap-shaped florets called ray flowers. These are female. The asters belong to the genus of the same name; *Aster* is Latin for star and hence they are often known as *starworts*.

Of the many species of asters that are found growing in the wild, the following are probably the ones that most of us are apt to see. The *large-leaved aster*, so called because of its broad, heart-shaped leaves, is a stout stiff purple stemmed species found in open woods and thickets. It has pale lavender or violet flower heads of about sixteen rays each. An easy aster to recognize is the *wavy-leaved aster* whose leaves have broad, winged stems. They are heart-shaped where they clasp the stem and have wavy margins. The flowers are pale blue to violet and often grow along one side of the stem. It is a species found in dry woods and on shaded roadsides.

A handsome aster, the *smooth or blue aster* has light-green lance-shaped leaves that are smooth to the touch and sky-blue or violet flower heads. It is common along woodland borders and roadsides during September and October.

Despite its rather local name, the *New England aster* is generally found throughout our range or throughout the eastern half of the country. It has a stout rigid stem that is bristly with stiff hairs; long blade-like, softly-haired toothless leaves; and numerous beautiful violet or magenta-purple flower heads that shine with royal splendor as much as six feet above the ground in swamps, meadows and wet thickets. One of the tallest of the asters, the *panicled white aster* is a bushy and coarse stemmed plant with dark green lance-shaped leaves and white, sometimes blue, or violet tinged flower heads. These are slightly larger than a nickel and grouped in loose or scattered clusters. This aster is rather common on low moist ground and in thickets. It is quite variable, differing in color, size of the ray flowers, and in leaf form.

One aster that everyone seems to know is the bushy little *white heath aster* or *Michaelmas daisy*, which may be found in fields and on roadsides. It has a smooth many-branched stem; tiny heath-like linear light-green leaves; and tiny white flowers with yellow disks that look like miniature daisies.

It is interesting to note that the *wavy-leaved aster* serves as a food plant for the caterpillars of the tawny crescent butterfly, the *New England aster* as a food plant for the caterpillars of the pearl crescent butterfly, and various asters as food plants for the caterpillars of the silvery checkerspot. Also, some birds eat the seeds and some mammals feed on the leaves.

Pliny wrote that a brew of asters was good for snakebite and that an amulet made of the plants was a panacea for sciatica. The religious order of the Shakers made a concoction of asters for the treatment of skin disorders.

Marsh Marigold

Golden cups by the brookside

There was a time when I would invariably go into the woods near where I lived, and where a brook whose rushing waters from melted snows coursed their way, whenever April reappeared on the calendar just to see once again the marsh marigolds huddling on little islands and opening their golden flowers. They are a festive board for bees and handsome flowerflies who show a liking for blossoms as gaily colored as their own brilliant bodies.

The marsh marigolds must have been plentiful in the meadows along the Avon during Shakespeare's time, for it is doubtless these were the flowers that inspired the musicians in *Cymbeline* to sing:

> *And winking Mary-buds begin*
> *To ope their golden eyes.*

The marsh marigold is not a true marigold nor even a cowslip as it is sometimes called. It is more of a buttercup. Its scientific name, *Caltha palustris*, means marsh cup—from *Caltha*, meaning cup, and *palus*, meaning marsh. The Indians called it *Onondaga—it blooms in the swamps*. The marsh marigold is a marshy plant, at home in swamps, low meadows, riverbanks, and even ditches. Its bright yellow flowers are a welcome relief from the dull hues of the early spring landscape. In the words of Tennyson, "the wild marsh marigold shines like fire in swamps and hollows gray."

The marsh marigold is a thick and hollow stemmed stocky plant with round or kidney-shaped deep-green leaves and brilliant golden-yellow flowers that resemble buttercups. These are cross-fertilized chiefly by the flowerflies. The leaves are often used as a potherb, especially in the spring or near the flowering season. They are boiled and served in the same way as spinach and many say they are equal, if not superior, to it. In some parts of the country the tender buds are pickled and used as a substitute for capers but they do not have the same piquancy.

The flowers are perfect with between five and nine petal-like sepals, have many stamens and pistils but no petals, and are rich in nectar. Although the anthers and stigmas mature at the same time, cross fertilization is favored because the anthers open outward and those farthest from the stigmas open first. They develop into many-seeded pods.

The origin of the word *marigold* is rather obscure. In the *Grete Herball* of the sixteenth century the flower is referred to as *Mary Gowles*, which in time became corrupted into *marigold*. In seventeenth-century slang *marigold*—or *marygold*—meant a sovereign.

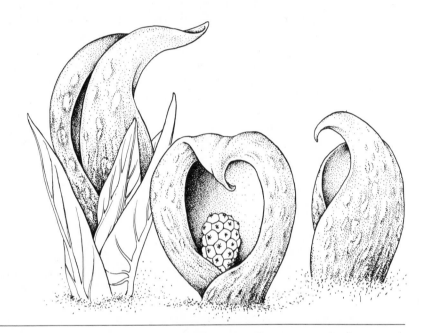

Skunk Cabbage
Hermits of the bog

It is generally agreed among botanists that the skunk cabbage is the first of our wildflowers to appear in the spring, though some may regard the hepatica as the first. The skunk cabbage may not evoke the same response as the hepatica but I have always had a special feeling for this perennial harbinger of spring, though its name does little to commend it to most of us who look for a more sophisticated kind of beauty. Although it may not be viewed as a floral delight, it is nevertheless unusual in form, interesting in character, and not entirely without redeeming qualities.

As early as January—sometimes even before—the skunk cabbage begins to push its pointed purplish shell-like leaf, which botanists call a *spathe*, above the moist earth. This will eventually unfold and curl about the tiny flowers, which are hidden from view. To some it appears rather gruesome and suggestive of a giant snail lifting itself above its muddy bed; yet its color pattern is not without aesthetic interest. As Mathews wrote in his *Fieldbook of American Wildflowers:* "the madder purple, green and yellow are blended and streaked with a peculiar charm; inside the red is darkest."

If some of us are bold enough to venture into certain swampy places in the still leafless woods and brown cheerless meadows of March where the skunk cabbage can be found, and if we are not deterred by its rather fetid odor from examining with a magnifying glass the tiny flesh-colored flowers which are profusely scattered over the stout and fleshy finger-like body which botanists call a *spadix*, we will discover that they are not unpleasing to the eye.

We are also likely to observe that the hive bees are among the first of the insects to visit this *hermit of the bog*, as the skunk cabbage has been called. But being ungrateful creatures they soon leave it alone when other, more attractive flowers appear. Perhaps it is just as well, for the hive bees never entered into the skunk cabbage's scheme of things. Many a bee that manages to gain entrance into the horn, manifestly designed for smaller insects, finds the going too slippery on its way out and falls back to perish miserably. However, small flies and gnats that have lived under the fallen leaves during the winter and gradually warmed into active life will soon swarm about the spathes.

Now Nature does not plan anything idly. The odor of the skunk cabbage—which combines a suspicion of skunk, putrid meat, and garlic—and the color pattern of the spathe, both of which resemble decaying flesh, are designed to attract those flies that, together with certain beetles, have the special mission in life of removing from the earth substances that, if left untouched, would pollute or contaminate. And so we soon find these small flies and gnats entering the shell-like leaf to crawl about the spadix, thus becoming covered with pollen that they will transport to another *hermit*, effecting cross-pollination.

After the flowering season is over the vivid green crowns of leaves begin to appear. When they have become completely unfolded they are one to two feet long and cabbage-like. It is said that the young leaves are good to eat when boiled to tenderness and seasoned with butter, pepper, and salt. By September the thick spathe has decayed and fallen away but the spadix has become an enlarged soft spongy singularly repellent looking mass of bright red berries. Each is about the size of a pea and each falls to the ground.

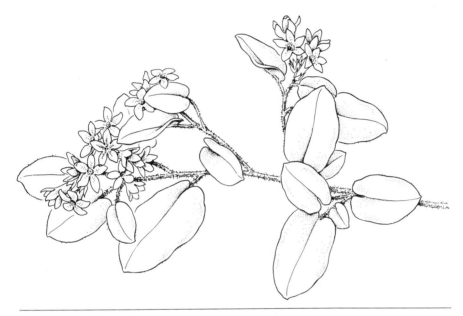

Trailing Arbutus
Of pilgrim devotion

The legend of the *Mayflower, trailing arbutus,* or *ground laurel,* as it is variously known, was given to us beautifully by Whittier in his poem "The Mayflowers." After the Pilgrims' first dreadful winter, this flower was the first to greet them and they took renewed hope and courage when they saw such a beautiful plant blossoming so bravely amid the winter snows: "O sacred flower of faith and hope."

Whether the association of the Mayflower with the Pilgrims and Plymouth Rock is correct or not is beside the point. Whether they named the plant because they first saw it during the month of May, as some have attempted to show, is equally unimportant, for certainly the Mayflower is not a typical May flower even in New England. Suffice that it is one of our earliest spring blossoms, a most charming plant and perhaps the most fragrant of our wildflowers. As Bryant said in his poem, "The Twenty-seventh of March":

> *Within the woods*
> *Tufts of ground laurel, creeping underneath   The leaves of last*
>   *summer,*
>   *send their sweets   Upon the chilly air. . . .*

The famed arbutus prefers dry ground, hillsides, and borders of rocky woods. It also grows in the vicinity of evergreens and it is in such places that I usually find its open chalices scenting the air of the spring woods with a delicious spicy fragrance that blends with the smell of pine and of damp soil being warmed to life. It seems a sacrilege, and in some states it is illegal, to pick the dainty blossoms that look as if they had been placed in our early spring woods as messengers of hope and gladness to those who have passed through a trying winter. That is how they must have appeared to the Pilgrims after that first winter on the bleak and rugged New England coast.

The trailing arbutus is something of a shrubby plant that stays close to the ground beneath a cover of decayed leaves. It has tough light-brown stems, old leaves of dull olive-green with rust colored spots, and new leaves that appear in June and that are lighter in color. These leaves have a rough surface and are netted with fine veins. They are evergreen. The flowers are white or delicately tinted pink, five lobed, and tubular. The calyx is constructed of five overlapping sepals. The flowers also have ten stamens, a pistil, and a five-lobed stigma. There are clusters of a few or many flowers at the ends of the branches. They are visited by the early queen bumblebees and eventually develop into capsules that split open revealing a whitish pulp covered with tiny seeds.

Dayflower

A tale of three brothers

Once upon a time there lived three brothers from Holland, whose name was Commelin. Two of them were botanists of repute who published their work; The third was also a botanist but lacked application and ambition and did not publish.

Now it so happens that there is a group of plants which we know as *dayflowers* whose blossoms have three petals—two blue and showy and the third white and inconspicuous. Linnaeus, the famed taxonomist, apparently decided one day while in a joking mood to place these flowers in a genus which he called *Commelina*, thus commemorating the three brothers. The two botanists of established reputation were represented by the two showy blue petals while the third, who failed to amount to anything in botany, was represented by the white inconspicuous petal. Happily this third brother died before the joke could be perpetuated in *Species Plantarum* and thus he was unaware of how the three brothers had become immortalized.

About our dooryards and in our gardens in the Northeast, the dayflower often takes possession of the soil to the exclusion of other plants. Elsewhere it may be found on riverbanks and in other wet, shady places. There are several species, essentially southern in range. Our northeastern species is a naturalized Asiatic that has extended its range as far as Texas. The flowers open only in the morning and close by noon. They are rather odd from a botanical point of view. The three sepals are unequal in size and so are the three petals. Two of the petals are rounded, showy, and blue while the other is inconspicuous and somewhat whitish. There are six stamens; three are fertile and one of these is bent inward. The other three are sterile and small.

The stem of the dayflower is rather fleshy, smooth, and mucilaginous. The leaves are generally lanced-shaped; those on the base of the stem have sheathing petioles and the floral ones are heart-shaped and folded to form a hood about the flowers. They are used as a potherb in foreign countries.

In the morning the flowers are open and because of the sharp erect bracts that lend them support they are alert and ready for a passing bee. Once the bees have visited the flowers and fertilized them the lovely petals roll up, never to open again, and quickly wilt into a wet, shapeless mass. Were we to touch it we would find a sticky blue fluid on our finger tips.

Forget-Me-Not

The last farewell

Who does not know the little forget-me-nots that grow on the wet grassy banks of brooks?

> *The sweet forget-me-nots*
> *That grow for happy lovers,*

as Tennyson would have it. But he seems to ignore the melancholy legend that tells of the lover who, when gathering some of the blossoms for his sweetheart, fell into a deep pool. As he was about to disappear from her sight forever, he threw a bunch of them on the bank calling out at the same time "forget me not."

The folk tale of the Persians as told by their poet Shiraz is happier:

> *It was in the golden morning of the early world, when an angel sat*
> *weeping outside the closed gates of Paradise. He had fallen from his*

high estate through loving a daughter of the earth, nor was he permitted to enter again until she whom he loved had planted the flowers of the forget-me-not in every corner of the world. He returned to earth and assisted her, and together they went hand in hand. When their task was ended, they entered Paradise together, for the fair woman, without tasting the bitterness of death, became immortal like the angel whose love her beauty had won when she sat by the river twining forget-me-nots in her hair.

I never seem to tire of looking for forget-me-nots by the brookside or in low meadows for when I find the exquisite little flowers I experience a sensation of inexpressible joy. I then relive the memory of another day. The true forget-me-not is a native of Eurasia, long cultivated in the garden but now an escape to wet places. It is a perennial with a slender, sprawling stem, somewhat hairy gray-green lance-shaped leaves that are either stemless or nearly so, and small light-blue flowers with a yellow eye. It was this golden eye—actually a golden ring around the flower's center—that led Herman Sprengel, the German botanist, to assume that the conspicuous markings at the entrance of many flowers serve as guide lines to the nectar wells for the insects. The forget-me-not, however, is not entirely dependent on insects, for it is able to set fertile seed without them.

Tall Meadow Rue

Starry plumy clusters

Towering above the surrounding vegetation and serenely blossoming among the many flowers that make the wet meadows of midsummer radiant with color, the starry, plumy clusters of the tall meadow rue may be seen from a distance, inviting us to take a closer look. Should we do so we would not be disappointed, for it is a lovely plant both in its soft feathery misty-white flowers and in its delicate foliage.

The tall meadow rue is a common plant in wet meadows, swamps, and brooksides where we find it blossoming from June to September and growing from three to ten feet tall. It has a stout light-green stem—possibly magenta tinged at the branches—leaves that are divided into lustreless olive-green leaflets, and decorative flower clusters that are often a foot long. The flowers lack petals and are polygamous; they may be male, female, or both on the same or on different plants. The female flowers have several pistils and usually some stamens. The male flowers have many erect thread-like stamens and are decidedly greenish-white in tone. Bees, the smaller butterflies, and moths visit the flowers and aid in cross-fertilization. However the tall meadow rue produces an over-abundance of light dry pollen that is easily carried by the wind, which is often an agent in cross-pollination as it is for the grasses and many trees.

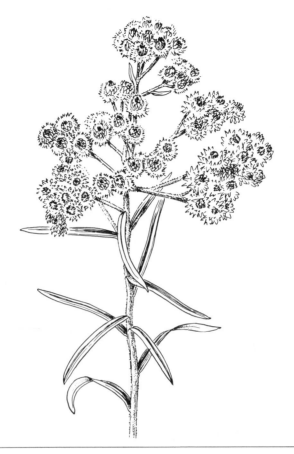

Pearly Everlasting

For a winter bouquet

Country women of yesteryear made winter bouquets and winter decorations of the pearly everlasting because of its lasting qualities. Hence its name. Perhaps they still do.

Neltje Blanchan, writing in *Nature's Garden*, said of the pearly everlasting:

> An imaginary blossom that never fades has been the dream of poets since Milton's day; but seeing one, who loves it. Our amaranth has the aspect of an artificial flower—stiff, dry, soulless, quite in keeping with the decorations on the average farmhouse mantelpiece. Here it forms the most uncheering of winter bouquets, or a wreath about flowers made from the lifeless hair of some dear departed.

The pearly everlasting is a densely woolly plant that we find blooming from July to September in old fields, dry pastures, waste places, and along the roadside. The stems—from one to three feet in height—as well as the leaves are profusely covered with hairs; the leaves have such a dense layer that all the veins except the midrib are hidden from view. Nonetheless it is a rather beautiful plant with leaves that are sage-green above and white beneath. The flowers are crowded in small terminal heads and miniature petal-like white scales surround the central yellow florets. The tiny florets—well protected in the center—are of two different kinds that are separated on distinct heads and self-fertilization under such an arrangement is impossible. And so the flowers are dependent on insect visitors: the moths and butterflies, though other insects also visit the flowers occasionally.

I don't know why but children of another day associated the pearly everlasting with graves. In writing of it Oliver Wendell Holmes said:

> *A something it has of sepulchral spicery, as if it had been brought from the core of some great pyramid, where it had lain on the breast of a mummied Pharaoh. Sometime, too, of immortality in the sad, faint sweetness lingering long in its lifeless petals. Yet this does not tell why it fills my eyes with tears, and carries me in blissful thought to the banks of asphodel that border the "River of Life."*

And Thoreau wrote of it:

> *The pearly everlasting is an interesting white at present. Though the stems and leaves are still green, it is dry unwithering like an artificial flower; its white, flexuous stem and branches, too, like wire wound with cotton. Neither is there any scent to betray it. Its amaranthine quality is instead of high color. Its very brown center now affects me as a fresh and original color. It monopolizes small circles in the midst of sweet fern, perchance on a dry hillside.*

Tall Bellflower

Of stately and handsome aspect

One of the more stately and handsome of our wildflowers, we find the tall bell-flower blooming throughout the summer in such places as moist, shady thickets, woodland borders, and damp grasslands. Its long slender wands, studded with blue or sometimes whitish flowers, wave high above the ground. And should we look closely at the flowers we might get the effect of miniature pinwheels in motion.

We should suspect from its name that it is a tall plant, as indeed it is; Its erect, slender rarely branched green stem at times attains a height of six feet but more commonly is only two or three feet tall. Its leaves are light- or dark-green, ovate to lance-shaped, toothed, and rather long and drooping and its flow-ers grow from the angles of the leaves in terminal clusters. Despite its common name and unlike most other bellflowers—of which there are some thousand to fifteen hundred species—the flowers are not bell-shaped but are usually flat. The corolla is about an inch broad and has five deep lobes spread nearly into a wheel-shape. The style curves downward and then upward, extending far beyond the mouth of the flower. If we approach the plant on a sunny day we must beware of the bees and the wasps known as yellow jackets which are its chief benefactors.

Yellow Meadow Lily

Fairy caps

Some years ago I became so enchanted with the *yellow meadow lily*—or *Canada lily* as it is perhaps better known since *Lilium canadense* is its botanical name— that I brought a few home and planted them in my garden. And I have had them ever since.

The Canada lily may not have the gorgeous coloring or subtle delicacy of some of the other lilies but it certainly has an unsurpassed grace and charm of its own, particularly evident in the graceful curves of its pendulous bells and un-excelled by any wild or cultivated flower. For this matchless quality it must al-ways command our greatest admiration.

The flowers of the Canada lily have been called *fairy caps* and also *witch caps*. The latter is perhaps more appropriate for the dainty headgear of the merry sprites of Wonderland.

The Canada lily is one of our few native species and is undoubtedly the most popular lily throughout our range. It is commonly found in wet meadows, sometimes in swamps, woodlands, and woodland borders, as well as in fields. Where it appears in profusion it tints such places with a golden color. Its stem ordinarily rises three feet in height and bears several whorls or circles of bright green lance-shaped leaves. Several flower stems extend from the main stem and each bears a delicate pendulous bell, dull buff-yellow or orange without and orange or pale-yellow within and speckled with dark reddish-brown or purple-brown spots. The pendulous position of the flower-cups protects the nectar from rain. This nectar is gathered mostly by the honey bee and the leaf-cutter bee, which also transport the brown pollen to other flowers and thus are effective in cross-pollination.

I can conceive of no more enchanting summer scene than a wood bordered meadow populated with the delicate nodding bells that appear to be ready to tinkle at the slightest disturbance.

Four-Leaved Loosestrife

A matter of symmetry

Quaint old Parkinson, an early English herbalist, in writing of the common wild loosestrife of Europe told us, "it is believed to take away strife, or debate between ye beasts, not only those that are yoked together, but even those that are wild also, by making them tame and quiet . . . if it be either put around their yokes or their necks, which how true, I leave to them shall try and find it soe." Our early colonists must have believed in the plant's virtues for it seems that they fed it to their oxen so that the animals would work together peacefully.

The loosestrife of which Parkinson wrote was once a garden favorite in our Eastern states but, long since having passed from favor, it made its escape and is now found in fields and along the roadsides. We have a number of native loosestrifes whose leaves, without marginal teeth, are variously arranged. Its flowers are solitary or in clusters, sometimes in the leaf axils or sometimes terminal, and bell- or wheel-shaped. It has a capsule for fruit.

The *four-leaved* or *whorled loosestrife* is a delicate and pretty species that is common in open woodlands, thickets, and roadsides. Since it blooms throughout the summer surely many of us have seen it but only as a passing acquaintance. It is a slender erect plant, one to three feet tall, with light-green lance-shaped pointed leaves. These leaves are generally arranged in a circle of four but sometimes they can be arranged in circles of three or six. When examined with a hand lens the leaves are seen to be covered with minute hairs. Slender long stems, each bearing a single star-shaped light-golden-yellow flower dotted with terra-cotta-red that often extends in faint streaks over the corolla lobes, project from the bases of the leaves. Both the male and female organs project from the bases of the leaves, and both project in a cone-shaped cluster, the female extending so far beyond the male that self-fertilization rarely occurs. Hence bumblebees and honey bees are its chief benefactors. The symmetry and bright coloring of the four-leaved loosestrife make it an attractive plant and most pleasing to the eye.

The genus to which the loosestrife belongs was named in honor of *Lysimachus*, a king of ancient Sicily, who is said to have used one of the loosestrifes to pacify a mad bull.

Oswego Tea

The Indians called it o-gee-chee

The Indians called it *O-Gee-Chee*, meaning *flaming flower*, but we know it as *oswego tea* or sometimes as *bee balm*. It is a brilliant and showy wildflower—exceeded in brilliance only by the cardinal flower—whose scarlet-red color, of a deeper red than most summer flowers, is strongly relieved by the background of shady woodland it grows against, in the wildwood tangles of mountain streams. We also find it in moist woods and thickets. It is a strong-growing perennial with a rather rough hairy square stem two feet or more in height. It has sombre dark-green opposite ovate to lance-shaped coarsely-toothed leaves. The smaller leaves just beneath the flowers are often tinged a ruddy color. The flowers are tubular, the calyx is sharply five-toothed, the corolla is two-lipped and five-lobed, the two long anther bearing stamens are ascending and protruding, and the pistil has a two-cleft style in a dense rounded terminal head-like cluster.

Although commonly visited by bees, the flowers are peculiarly adapted

55

to the visits of butterflies, the common sulphur and the monarch being the most frequent visitors. The ruby-throated hummingbird also may be seen frequently, flashing about these Indian plumes. Like the insects, it transfers pollen on its needle-like bill as it darts from flower to flower.

The plant got its name from the fact that the Oswego Indians of New York brewed a tea from the leaves. The early colonists are said to have done the same. As the plant has a strong mint flavor—it is a member of the mint family—it is sometimes used in cooking and is frequently mentioned in lists of pot-herbs and sweet herbs. As a point of further interest, it belongs to the genus *Monarda* which was named after Nicholas Monardes. He was a Spanish author of many tracts on medicinal and other useful plants, especially those of the New World, during the latter half of the sixteenth century. He published a book in 1571 containing the earliest picture of an American plant.

Wild Senna

A look of elegance

Were we to stroll along almost any roadside in midsummer our attention might very well be attracted by bright golden-yellow flower clusters, the flowers accentuated in color by the prominent chocolate-brown of the anthers, which contrasts sharply with the deep green of the beautiful foliage. And if we are sensitive to the aesthetic we are likely to pause and remark that here is a plant with a look of elegance—as if it cared for its own appearance.

The wild senna—we also find it growing in alluvial or moist rich soil and in swamps, and sometimes even in pastures and meadows—is a decorative and showy perennial with stems three to four feet or more in height and with leaves composed of between twelve and eighteen broad lance-shaped smooth leaflets. These are dark-green above and paler below and somewhat sensitive to the touch. The flowers have a calyx of five lobes, five unequal petals, and ten yellow stamens. Three of the lobes of the calyx are close together at the top, while the other two, which are larger and broader, are below. The stamens have filaments of differing lengths and are tipped with brown anthers of differing sizes. The three lowest stamens are the largest. The flowers are together in many loose clusters and are either axial or terminal. They develop into pods that are about three inches long, flat, and curved. They eventually turn to a dark red-dish-brown.

The caterpillars of the cloudless sulphur, the orange barred sulphur, the sleepy orange, and the little sulphur butterflies all use the wild senna as a food plant. Grazing animals leave the plant undisturbed or, if forced to browse the leaves by a lack of forage, they suffer *scours* because it has a strong cathartic action. The leaflets, stripped from their stalks at flowering time and carefully dried, have been sold in the drug market for their medicinal qualities.

Common Speedwell

A darling blue

According to legend, when Jesus was on his way to Calvary he faltered as he passed the home of a Jewish maiden. This maiden, when she saw the drops of agony on his face, ran out to him and wiped his face with her kerchief. Forever after, according to the monks, the kerchief bore the impress of his features: *vera iconica—the true likeness.*

Later, when the Church canonized her, the maiden was given the name of St. Veronica. This is an abbreviated form of the Latin words. Her kerchief became one of the most priceless relics of the Roman Church.

In the course of time the people of the Middle Ages, in their imagination, came to believe that they saw a resemblance to the relic in the wildflower that we know today as the *common speedwell* and so they gave the plant the saint's name. Moreover, as the piece of pictured linen was believed to have healing virtues and as Rome was far away and few could travel there to be cured by it, they turned to the plant believing that it too might have healing qualities. The people's belief was so strong that it actually did appear to have miraculous powers.

The common speedwell is a native of the United States, the British Isles, and Eurasia and is common in dry fields, wooded hillsides, open woods, pastures, waste places, and also, occasionally, on our lawns. This is the flower of which Tennyson said, "the little speedwell's darling blue," and in *A Glance at British Flowers* John Burroughs wrote that "it is prettier than the violet and larger and deeper colored than our houstonia. It is a small and delicate edition of our hepatica, done in indigo blue, and wonted to the grass and in the fields and wastesides."

The common speedwell is a woolly species with prostrate stems, three to ten inches long, that finally become erect and light-green oval to elliptical leaves, with spike-like flower clusters of pale-lavender striped with light-violet or dark-blue.

The flowers are tiny, being only about a quarter of an inch broad. Each is a little disk cut into four lobes with the lowest lobe being the smallest. Only when the common speedwell grows in masses does it become conspicuous and to the insects it then becomes a living advertisement for its nectar.

The plant is a medicinal herb and was once collected, dried, and sold in shops for its reputed diuretic and astringent properties.

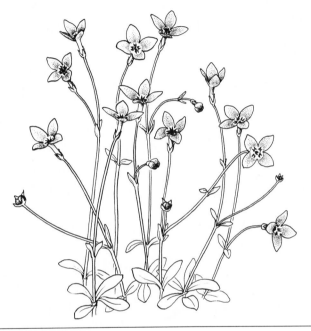

Bluets

A milky path of tiny floral stars

To my way of thinking one of the most delightful of the early spring flowers is the *bluet*, also known as the *houstonia, Quaker-ladies,* and *innocence.* By itself it is not a showy flower but when massed together in countless numbers the bluets trace a milky path beautiful to see in fields and meadows and along the waysides. As Blanchan wrote, they reflect the "blue and serenity of heaven in their, pure, upturned faces."

> *Innocents, children, guileless and frail,*
> *Meek little faces, upturned and pale.*

So wrote Harriet L. Keeler in "Our Early Wildflowers." Where we find the white variety growing we might well believe that a light snowfall has dusted the grass to form a terrestrial path of tiny floral stars.

The bluet is a perennial and forms dense mats of oblong lance-shaped tiny light-green root leaves. It has slender thread-like stems with a few small opposite leaflets. These stems bear funnel-shaped flowers with four pointed petal-like lobes that may be light-blue, pale-lilac, or nearly white with golden-yellow centers.

An interesting feature of this plant is that there are two kinds of flowers. These, strangely enough, do not occur in the same patch—a phenomenon that botanists call dimorphism. In other words, the flowers in one patch may be female with abortive male organs whereas in another patch they may be male with abortive female organs. The reason for the two kinds of flowers is to secure cross-pollination. Thus an insect visiting the flowers of one patch will become dusted with pollen that will be transported to the flowers of another patch. The converse also holds true.

The bluets have many benefactors but the principal ones are the small bees and butterflies. Among the latter are the clouded sulphur, the painted lady, and the common meadow fritillary, which we often may see moving its tawny dark speckled wings rhythmically in apparent ecstasy as it sips from each dainty nectar cup. Flies and beetles also visit the blossoms but the small bees are best adapted for ensuring cross-pollination.

The bluets appear from April to July and then sparsely throughout the summer. A pot of roots gathered in the fall and placed in a sunny window will likely produce a little colony of flowers throughout the winter.

Frostweed

Of ice crystals

In its own manner the frostweed is as unique as any flower you will find. It is an erect plant, about a foot tall, with lance-oblong dull-green leaves that are hoary with fine hair on the lower surface. It has two kinds of flowers; The early ones are solitary, an inch or so broad, and have showy yellow petals. There are five wedge-shaped petals, five unequal sepals, and many stamens. The later flowers are small, abundant, and lack petals and are clustered at the bases of the leaves.

The frostweed thrives in dry fields and sandy places. The solitary flowers open for only a day—and the day must be a bright and sunny one. The petals fall the next day, having served their purpose. The stamens also drop but the club-shaped pistil, having been dusted with sufficient pollen, remains to develop into a rounded ovoid pod. The first flower is succeeded by a second one, the second is succeeded by a third, and so the succession continues for weeks. Then, as summer begins to wane, smaller flowers without petals appear and produce pods that are no larger than pinheads.

The plant ends its blooming before the first frosts of autumn. Why, then, is it called the frostweed? Examine the plant on some cold November morning, if you are a hardy soul, and you will find, around the base of the stem or in the cracked bark of the root, ice crystals that might easily be mistaken for bits of glistening quartz. These are formed from the sap that oozes out and freezes solid. At times the frozen sap assumes a feathery whimsical form that stimulates the imagination.

Tansy

Yellow buttons by the wayside

Of the tansy, Gerarde wrote: "In the spring time, are made with the leaves thereof newly sprung up, and with eggs, cakes or Tansies which be pleasant in taste and goode for the Stomache." Tansies were popular in the seventeenth century for Samuel Pepys wrote of them in his diary. In describing a dinner for some guests he wrote that "it consisted of a brace of stewed carps, six roasted chickens, and a jowl of salmon, hot, for the first course; two neat's tongues, cheese, and a tansy for the second." The *tansy* was a kind of cake or fritter made from the leaves of the plant. It is written in *Cole's Art of Simpling*, published in 1656, that maidens were assured that tansy leaves laid to soak in buttermilk for nine days "maketh the complexion very fair." According to the medieval herbalists, a tea made from tansy leaves was a cure for every human ill. At any rate, until recently tansy tea was a favorite beverage for colds and similar ailments in this country; perhaps it still is.

The tansy is one of the more common plants of summer. Its rather flat, clustered dull orange-yellow flower heads are a familiar sight along roadsides, in fields, and in waste places. The flowers look like those of the daisy without the white rays. The inner florets are both male and female, with the marginal ones being female. As a matter of fact the flowers are very button-like and hence the tansy is sometimes known as *bitter buttons.* An immigrant from Europe and an escape from garden cultivation, the tansy is a rather rank growing herb, two to three feet in height, with alternate ornamentally toothed and cut leaves. They are strongly aromatic.

For centuries the tansy was used medicinally to effect abortions, often with fatal results. The leaves and stem contain tanacetum, an oil that is toxic to humans and animals. But somewhat surprisingly perhaps, the fresh young leaves and flowers can be used as a substitute for sage in cooking.

Black-Eyed Susan
Merry maidens

Unlike the female ray florets of the daisy, the orange-yellow ray florets of the black-eyed Susan are neutral; that is, they have neither stamens nor pistils. However, the purplish-brown florets that form the conical disk are perfect. In other words, they are both male and female, staminate and pistillate. The florets at the base of the disk open first and their pollen forms a yellow circle. Then the next higher florets on the disk open, forming another yellow circle, and this continues as blossoming circles climb toward the apex. Sometimes small caterpillars are found in the heads of the black-eyed Susan and they have the habit of attaching small pieces of the flowers to their backs, keeping them in place with silk. No doubt this helps them by acting as a bit of camouflage helps in concealment.

Unlike so many of our wild plants, which landed on eastern shores and marched westward, the black-eyed Susan is a western species that travelled eastward, supposedly in bundles of hay. It is a plant one to three feet in height, with very rough and bristly stems and leaves. The stem is exceedingly tough and the leaves are dull olive-green, lance-shaped, toothless or nearly so, and scattered along the stem. The lower leaves have three prominent veins and winged leaf-stalks. By the middle of July our dry meadows are alive with hundreds of these merry maidens, in a carnival mood alongside yellow lilies and brilliant milk-weeds.

Common Meadow Buttercup

Every child's favorite

"The flowery May," wrote Milton of the fifth month of the year. No one can dispute the poet, for during this month many colorful and different sized flowers and blossoms appear on the landscape. They may be seen in field and meadow, in the thicket and woodland, along the roadside and brookside, by the edge of pond and stream, and even in the water itself. If there is any one flower which we can truly associate with May, it is probably the buttercup. This association can be traced back to childhood days when the bright yellow blossoms were a special delight and every child's favorite. When

cuckoo buds of yellow hue
Do paint the meadows with delight.

And what child of yesteryear did not hold the shining golden blossoms under his chin to test his fondness for butter?

The genus name of the buttercup is *Ranunculus* and is from the Latin for *little frog*—an allusion to the wet places where buttercups tend to grow. Although there are some species that prefer moist habitats, others are common in the woods, fields, and roadside banks.

There isn't anything complex about a buttercup's blossom. It has five pale-yellow sepals with brownish tips that were green in the bud, five petals that are bright yellow above and pale beneath and that shine as if they were varnished, numerous stamens, and several pistils. Each petal is wedge-shaped with its broad outer edge curved to form a cup-like flower. If a petal were removed and examined under a magnifying glass, a small scale would be seen at its base. It covers the nectariferous pit.

A newly opened buttercup reveals the anthers huddled in the center. Later they form a fringy ring about the pale green pistils, each pistil having a short yellowish stigma—the part that receives the pollen. It is interesting to note that the anthers open away from the pistils to prevent self-fertilization and also that they shed much of their pollen before the stigmas are ready to receive it. The smaller bees, butterflies, flowerflies, wasps, and beetles visit the flowers and serve as agents of cross-fertilization. Later the flowers become a tiny cluster of dry fruits called *achenes.*

There are several species of buttercups and all have tuberous or fibrous roots; simple or compound leaves that are often cut, lobed, or divided; and flowers that are prevailingly yellow. The *common meadow buttercup*—the familiar buttercup of fields and meadows—is an immigrant from Europe with a hairy, branched deep-green stem that is two to three feet tall. It has deep green leaves with between three and seven stemless divisions that are cleft into several narrow pointed lobes in a most decorative manner. The flowers, on long slender stems, sometimes continue to bloom until the first frost. Both the stem and leaves contain a peculiarly acrid juice that will cause blisters if applied to the skin and that is poisonous if eaten. Children should be warned against biting into the stem or leaves. Cattle are aware of the plant's toxic character and shun it.

Showy Tick Trefoil

By hook or by crook

When one travels about the country and sees the same plants growing here and there—often in rather remote areas—he or she may often wonder how they ever got there in the first place. It is no mystery however, for plants have devised many ways to effect a distribution of their seeds. Some, like the thistles and dandelions, have designed silken parachutes. Others, like the maples and ashes have designed wings and darts. These are carried near and far by the wind. Others creep along the ground at a tortoise's pace. But as in the fable that pace a winning one. Still others have enclosed their seeds in bright and fleshy berries that attract the birds who deposit the seeds in distant places. Wasn't it Darwin who raised over sixty wild plants from seeds carried in a pellet of mud taken from the leg of a partridge? And then there are those whose seeds are furnished with hooks and barbs that catch in the fur of animals and thus receive free transportation to places far from their place of origin: plants such as the tick trefoils for instance.

There are many species of *tick trefoils*. They are of the genus *Desmodium*, from the Greek for *chain* in reference to the jointed pods. They are somewhat weedy plants—viewed indifferently by gardeners—with characteristics of the pea family; namely, they have compound leaves of usually three leaflets, small and pea-like flowers, and a prominently jointed pod with the segments that become detached separately and often catch in our clothing, as well as in the fur of various animals. How often I have walked through the woods only to find my clothing covered with hundreds of the little pods that have stolen a ride in the hope of being dropped amid conditions more favorable for raising a family.

One of the more common of the tick trefoils is the *naked-flowered tick trefoil*. It grows in woods where it lifts its narrow clusters of a few rose-purple flowers about two feet above the ground. These flowers are fertilized by the honeybees and mining bees. The caterpillars of such butterflies as the eastern-tailed blue and hoary edge find the leaves much to their taste.

The pointed-leaved tick trefoil has a unique distinguishing feature. It has a cluster of leaves high up on a stem, from which a stalk bearing a number of purple flowers also arises. These flowers are larger than those of the preceding species. They appear in June and may be seen until September in dry or rocky woods.

Unlike either of the two preceding species, the *prostrate tick trefoil* lies outstretched on the dry ground of open woods and copses. It is between two and six feet in length. The others have erect stems between two and three feet tall. In addition to its habit of lying prostrate, it can easily be recognized by its almost perfectly round leaflets, by its rather loose clusters of deep-purple flowers, and by its three to five jointed pod, which is deeply scalloped on its lower edge.

The *showy* or *Canadian tick trefoil* is undoubtedly the most showy of all the various tick trefoils one is likely to find on outdoor rambles. Its flowers are larger than those of the others, vary in color from magenta to magenta-pink, and crowd in clusters that terminate a tall, stout, and hairy stem. Its leaves are nearly without stalks and the three leaflets are oblong lance-shaped. It is common in moist open woods, along the edges of fields, on the borders of copses, and along river banks.

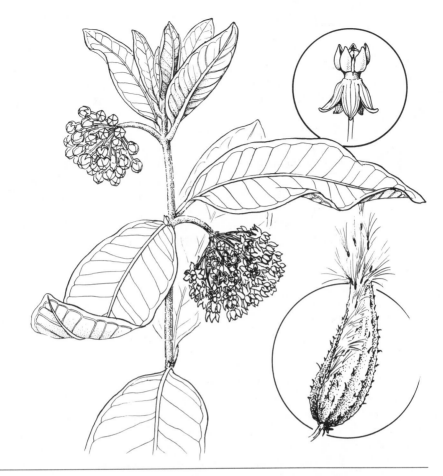

Common Milkweed

A festive board

Nearly everyone is familiar with the common milkweed. With its cloyingly sweet, somewhat pendulous flower clusters it is one of the more familiar of our summer wildflowers and from June to September it is found blossoming along roadsides and in fields and waste places. Its richly nectar-laden flowers are a veritable banquet table for all kinds of flying insects.

A native perennial, it grows from three to five feet tall. It has a stout, sturdy stem and light yellow-green oblong leaves in opposite pairs. These taper at both ends and are very finely haired. It has numerous dull pale greenish-purple-pink, brownish-pink, pale-lavender-brown, crimson-pink, or even yellowish flowers. The flowers are perfect—both male and female—and have five sepals that are separate or nearly so; a five-lobed or five-parted corolla, the lobes usually bent backwards; five male organs or stamens, the filaments usually united into a column; a crownlike organ—*corona*—usually between the stamens and petals;

and two female organs or *pistils*. The anthers and stigma are connected remarkably and the pollen coheres in waxy or granular pear-shaped masses—*pollinia*—that often become attached to the feet of insects, sometimes ensuring their death.

The pollinia are designed so that when an insect steps upon the edge of the flower to sip nectar its legs slip between the peculiarly shaped nectariferous hoods situated in front of each anther. As it then draws its leg upward a claw, hair, or spine catches in a v-shaped fissure and is guided along a slit to a notched disk that becomes attached to the leg. Since the pollinia are each connected to the disk by a stalk they are carried off when the insect leaves. Upon the insect's arrival at another milkweed flower the pollinia are easily introduced into the stigmatic chamber. The struggle of the insect at this time breaks the stalk of the pollinia and the insect is relieved of its load. Sometimes an insect loses a leg or is permanently entrapped.

In the course of time the flowers develop into two thick warty pods that split open on one side when mature, releasing many yellow-brown seeds. Each seed has a tuft or parachute of silky white fluffy hairs that catch in the wind. The seeds are a familiar sight sailing through the air in early autumn. They also float on water so, lacking transportation by the wind, they can still obtain wide distribution.

The common milkweed is distasteful and grazing animals leave it alone as a rule but sometimes the leaves are eaten and poisoning results. This often proves fatal, with sheep seeming to be the most susceptible. What may seem rather strange in view of the nature of the leaves and stem is that the plant is good as a potherb. If collected when young and tender—that is, when only a few inches high—and cooked like asparagus, the crisp succulent shoots make an excellent "dish of greens." The leaves have a taste somewhat like that of spinach after being cooked. It is said that a good brown sugar can be made from the flowers and John Fremont, the American explorer and soldier, related that the Indians of the Platte River country cooked the pods with buffalo meat.

The common milkweed is the chief, indeed, practically the only, food plant of the monarch butterfly and during the summer the caterpillars, with their alternate bands of yellow, black, and white, may be found feeding on the leaves.

Mayapple
The umbrellas are out

When the leaves of the mayapple, remarkable for their size and poisonous quality and frequently measuring a foot in diameter, first unfold in the spring like tiny umbrellas the children of another generation used to cry "the umbrellas are out." The curious leaves betray the hiding place of the ill-smelling but handsome white flower that measures nearly two inches wide.

We find the mayapple not only in the open woods but also along fences and roadsides. Its long horizontal rootstalks are poisonous and remain in the ground year after year, each spring sending up a one- or two-leaved plant twelve to eighteen inches tall. The one-leaved plant is flowerless and has a single leaf with seven to nine lobes. It is shield-shaped and, like an umbrella, supported by the stem in the center. The two-leaved plant has two symmetrical leaves that are somewhat smaller and attached to the two forks of the stem by their inner edges. The flower, which usually has six petals and twice as many stamens, droops from between the two forks of the stem. Though it has no nectar it is nevertheless cross-fertilized by early bees and bumblebees. Despite its poisonous character the mayapple is included in the dietary of the variegated fritillary, the leaves being eaten by the caterpillars.

There are some people who like the fruit of the mayapple, finding it to have a sweetish strawberry flavor, while others consider it to have a mawkish taste. The Indians valued it for medicinal purposes. The mayapple is a handsome woodland plant and it is also known as the *wild lemon* in allusion to its peculiar lemon-like fruit. This fruit is a large yellowish egg-shaped many-seeded berry.

Yarrow

A warrior's balm

One of the more conspicuous and familiar wildflowers of the midsummer scene is the yarrow. Few plants have as great a worldwide distribution as the yarrow and few appear so often in mythology, folklore, and literature. Chiron the Centaur is said to have named the yarrow after Achilles—its scientific name is *Achillae Millefolium*—who is supposed to have used it to heal his wounded soldiers at the siege of Troy. Old books list its virtues, describing it as a love charm, a cure-all for diverse ailments, and an ingredient in an intoxicating drink. The early English botanists called the plant *nose-bleed* "because the leaves being put into the nose caused it to bleed." And Gerarde wrote that "most men say that the leaves chewed, and especially greene, are a remedie for the toothache." These same pungent leaves led to the plant being called *old man's pepper*, and a beer made from the leaves in Sweden led Linnaeus to remark that it was more intoxicating than one made from hops. In the Orkney Islands the old women regarded *milfoil tea* as most efficacious for dispelling melancholia and in Switzerland an excellent vinegar is said to have been made from an Alpine species. Finally, in England it was believed at one time that if a spray of yarrow were placed beneath a pillow on Midsummer's Eve the sleeper would dream of his or her future wife or husband. As an old rhyme had it:

> *Thou pretty herb of Venus tree*
> *Thy true name it is Yarrow*
> *Now who my dearest friend shall be*
> *Pray tell thou me to-morrow.*

Aesthetically, the yarrow has mixed qualities. The feathery masses of finely dissected leaves have a lacelike character that is appealing to the eye but its dusty-looking flat-topped flower clusters of small grayish-white or white flowers give it a sort of unkempt appearance. When viewed with a hand lens the individual flowers belie their collective appearance and are not unattractive. The perfect disk florets are at first yellow but later turn brown. The female ray flowers are a white or grayish-white or, in some rare cases, crimson-pink. The flowers are fertilized mostly by bees and the smaller butterflies. Chief among these is the common or clouded sulphur.

An immigrant from Europe, we find the yarrow growing in dry fields, along the roadside, in waste places, and on banks. It is from one to two feet tall. Were we to examine a flower cluster we would most likely find two dissimilar animals lying in ambush. One would be a small white crab-like spider and the other a greenish-yellow insect with a broad black band across the expanded part of the abdomen. The spider is of unusual interest because later in the summer it moves to a yellow flower and turns yellow and spiders, as a rule, do not change color. The insect is called the ambush bug and is well named. Both the rather grotesque form of the body and its peculiar coloring simulate the blossoms among which it hides, helping to conceal it.

Night-Flowering Catchfly

Beacons in the night

As dusk begins to settle over the fields and woods on a summer's day and as the night-flying moths begin to make their rounds the night-flowering catchfly opens its white or pinkish blossoms which, by their fragrance, serve as beacons of the night. They direct the moths to where a feast has been prepared for them alone. Sticky hairs along the stems ruthlessly destroy flies, ants, and other pilferers that would steal the nectar without rendering any service in return.

Once cultivated in gardens because of its fragrance and beauty but long since an escape, we find the night-flowering catchfly in fields and meadows and waste places everywhere. Its stem is erect and rather stout, growing one to three feet in height. Its basal and lower leaves are three to five inches long and somewhat spatulate; its upper leaves are sessile and ovate to lance-shaped; its flowers are in spreading clusters with five deeply cleft petals that open at twilight and close again at sunrise; its calyx is beautifully marked and resembles spun glass; it has ten stamens and three styles. The flowers later develop into ovoid capsules that contain many grayish-brown seeds.

In his *Familiar Flowers of Field and Garden,* F. Schuyler Mathews wrote, in speaking about the night-flowering catchfly:

> *It blooms side by side with the evening primrose, and might easily be taken for a white variety of the latter flower by one who consults his imagination rather than his botany. This catchfly is the most beautiful thing imaginable under the magnifying glass; the petals are not so remarkable, but the calyx (the protecting green envelope of the flower) is as delicate as though it were modeled in spun glass, the translucent line of green and white, the symmetry of the tiny form, are all worth the closest examination. If the plant had been formed of the most fragile and delicately colored glass it could scarcely have been more curious or beautiful.*

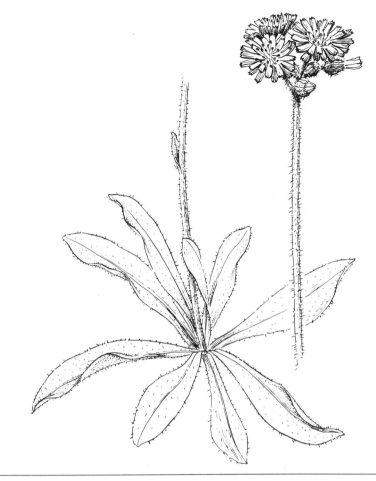

Devil's Paintbrush

Fields afire

When the devil's paintbrush begins to open its flaming orange-red flowers, the fields, woods, roadsides, and waste places appear from a distance as if they were on fire. And needless to say, the mining bees, flies, and the smaller butterflies such as the cabbage butterfly and the common sulphur, for whom such splendor was designed, are attracted to the brilliant flowers no less than are we.

The *devil's paintbrush*, or more prosaically, the *orange* or *tawny hawk-weed*, is an odd but attractive plant. It has a stout unbranched stem that is seven to sixteen inches tall and a flower cup covered with sepia-brown hairs that led the people in England of many years ago to call it *Grim the Collier* after a comedy with the same name that was popular during the reign of Queen Elizabeth.

In his *Herbal* Gerarde wrote: "The stalkes and cups of the floures are all set thicke with a blackish downe or hairiness as if it were the dust of coals, whence the women, who keep it in their gardens for novelties sake, have named it Grim the Collier . . . This is a stranger and only to be found in some few gardens."

The leaves are coarse, blunt, lance-shaped, and covered with short gray hairs and are nearly all at the base of the plant. The flowers, strap-rayed and finely fringed at the edges, are tawny-orange with light golden pistils and are grouped in small terminal clusters. However only a few of these flowers open at a time.

After cross-fertilization has occurred a single row of slender brownish persistent bristles that are attached to the seeds transform the head into the *Devil's paintbrush*. By means of the tiny parachutes the seeds are carried far and wide by the winds. An immigrant perennial from Europe, it is a pernicious weed that grazing animals dislike intensely because it is densely hairy and also because its juices are acrid and bitter. At one time it was believed by the people of the old world that hawks improved their eyesight with the leaves of a plant that they finally came to call the *hawkweed*. When transplanted to the garden the orange or tawny hawkweed will form a spreading mass of unusual color.

Moccasin Flower

The exquisite

Of all our native lady slippers the *moccasin flower*, or *stemless lady slipper*, is supposed to be the most common. I am not sure that this is so any longer as many thoughtless people have picked it indiscriminately and it is rapidly vanishing from the scene. But were we to follow almost any woodland trail in May or June we might, if we were lucky, find it amidst the brown carpet of the woodland floor, swinging balloon-like in the murmuring wind:

> *Graceful and tall the slender drooping stem*
> *With two broad leaves below*
> *Shapely the flower so lightly poised between*
> *And warm her rosy glow.*

This exquisite flower, almost too beautiful to be found in the moist woods, has an undefinable charm that never seems to wane. It seems to have been touched with the spirit of the woods and, as its Indian name suggests, it almost looks as if it came directly from the home of the red man.

The moccasin flower is so distinctive that we can hardly fail to recognize it. It has two basal ovalish leaves from the root. These are dark green above, with silvery hair beneath. It also has a solitary somewhat fragrant flower at the end of a long scurfy-haired stem. The pouch or lip of the flower is crimson-pink and veined with a deeper pink. The sepals and petals are greenish and brown.

And if we were to find the moccasin flower we might well observe how ingeniously it compels insects to carry its pollen. For once an insect has feasted in the large banquet chamber it must first rub along the sticky overhanging stigma with its rigid sharply pointed papillae that comb out the pollen it has brought from another flower. Then it must pass an anther that, being drawn downward on a hinge, covers the insect with more pollen before it can emerge out into the open. The flower is best adapted to the smaller bees, the honey bees and the mining bees, for sometimes a bumblebee will become imprisoned in it and must either bite its way out or perish miserably in its gorgeous prison.

Wood Anemone

The essence of spring

I doubt if there is a plant more typical of early spring or one that exudes the essence of spring more than the *wood anemone* or *windflower*, whose tremulous star-like blossoms quiver in the slightest breeze along the woodland border and on shaded hillsides. And I also doubt if any plant shows a more perfect adaptation to its environment.

It has a slender, though tough and pliable, stem that the strongest winds cannot break and a horizontal rootstalk that firmly anchors it in the ground. Its solitary white flower has many stamens and carpels and many petal-like sepals that do the advertising for insects. It has no corolla. The flower is set off by a background of whorled deep-green leaves: the better to advertise its wares to the insects that visit it. The flower also nods in cloudy weather—a refinement to ensure fertilization by wind carried pollen in case insects fail to supply it. Thus the charming wood anemone is as well equipped for survival in the

85

endless struggle for existence as is the more familiar and highly successful dandelion.

> *Within the woods*
> *whose young and half transparent leaves scarce cast*
> *A shade, gay circles of anemones*
> *Dance on their stalks,*

wrote Bryant, vividly bringing before us the feathery foliage of the spring woods
and the delicate beauty of the long stemmed anemones.

The word anemone comes from the Greek word meaning *wind*. According to one poetic Greek tradition, *Anemos—the wind*—used the little star-
like namesakes to announce his coming in early spring. And Pliny declares that
only the wind could open anemones. Bion, the bucolic Greek poet, had this to
say:

> *As many drops as from Adonis bled*
> *So many tears the sorrowing Venus shed*
> *For every drop on earth a flower there grows*
> *Anemones for tears, for blood the rose.*

He was referring to Venus' grief over the death of her youthful lover, Adonis.

At one time it was believed that the wind that passed over a field of
anemones was poisoned and that disease would soon follow in its wake. Certain
European peasants were known to run past a colony of these plants in the belief
that the air was tainted by them. Most likely it was because of this superstition
that the Persians adopted the flower as an emblem of sickness. And yet the
Romans ceremonially picked the first anemone of the year, using an incantation
that was believed to guard them against fever. At one time the very same plant
that grows in our woods, which also occurs in Asia, was planted on graves by the
Chinese who called it the *death flower*.

In a letter dated May 1, 1841 Nathaniel Hawthorne wrote to his
fiancee:

> *My cold has almost entirely departed . . . but as the ground is so*
> *damp, and the atmosphere so chill, I intend to keep myself on the*
> *sick-list this one day longer, more especially as I wish to read Carlyle*
> *on Heroes . . . There has been but one flower found in this vicinity—*
> *and that was an anemone, a poor, pale, shivering little flower, that*
> *had crept under a stonewall for shelter.*

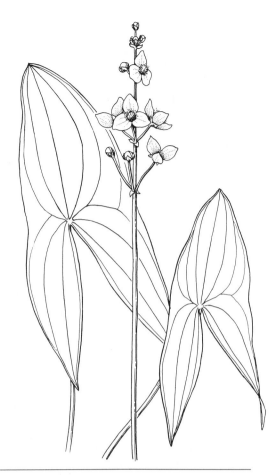

Arrowhead

In the mold of hecate

If any of us should study the edge of a pond we would find that the plants that grow in the water do not grow haphazardly but in clearly defined zones. Thus we would find the emergent water plants near the shore: bulrushes, burweeds, reeds, marsh grasses, white-blossomed arrowheads, arrow arums, water plantains, massed blue spikes of the pickerel weed, and tall phalanxes of cattails crowding every nook and corner. These are all plants that have their roots in water but their stems, leaves, and flowers in the air, with the submerged parts of their stems covered with the simple desmids and diatoms.

Then farther out where the water is knee deep or a little deeper we would see the deep aquatics with floating leaves—the water lily, the spatterdock or yellow water lily, and the water smartweed with its rose colored flowers. Here, too, we would see the free floating duckweeds and just below the surface the little vine-like liverwort and bladderwort. In still deeper water we would observe the ribbon-like leaves of the pondweeds and the freshwater eelgrass streaming upward from the bottom. This is the zone of submerged water plants: meadows of waterweeds, stoneworts, and water crowfoots, the latter with finely dissected leaves. These leaves are little more than forked hairs that spread out in dainty patterns when seen beneath the surface but collapse and become a soggy mass when lifted out of the water.

How these plants are adapted to live in water may be seen by observing the arrowhead. Looking carefully we should find a plant with broad arrow-like leaves, another with broad ribbon-like leaves, and a third with narrow grass-like leaves, though they may grow only a few inches apart. We might even find one with all three kinds of leaves. But though they may grow only a few inches apart they occur at varying depths. Hence, it would seem to follow that variation in the width of leaves must be correlated with depth of water. The arrowhead growing in the deepest water must have narrow grass-like leaves that bring the greatest possible surface area in contact with the air dissolved in the water and yet can glide harmlessly through the water: broad leaves would be torn to shreds by the water currents. Then, as the water becomes progressively more shallow, the grass-like leaves are discarded for the more broadly ribboned ones. These in turn give way to the conventional broad arrow-like leaves that are more suited to functioning in the air when the plant grows along the margin of the pond. Hence, the arrowhead is able to adjust itself to varying degrees of water depth, to drought or flood, and can live in and out of water with all the facility of a frog. We might almost say that the arrowhead has been caste in the mold of Hecate who, as you may recall, was represented as a triple goddess. Sometimes she had three heads—one of a horse, one of a dog, and one of a boar—and sometimes three bodies, standing back to back. And as goddess of a lower world she became the goddess of magic, ghosts, and witchcraft. Shakespeare refers to her triple character when he writes:

> *And we fairies that do run*
> *By the triple Hecate's team.*

There are a number of species of arrowheads. Typically, they are smooth, nearly always with arrow-shaped leaves and an erect flower-stalk that has three-petaled white flowers in circles of threes. They grow in the quiet waters of streams and on the margin of ponds.

Various agents distribute the pollen of the arrowhead. Not the least of these are the insects that frequent wet places such as the beautiful glassy-winged dragonfly.

Turtlehead

A reptilian facsimile

I don't believe that it requires a great deal of imagination to invest the flower of the turtlehead with reptilian features. This smooth-stemmed plant has deep-green toothed lance-shaped leaves and white flowers that are delicately tinged magenta-pink or crimson-pink. They are not unlike a turtle's head. The plant sometimes grows three feet tall in swamps, along the brookside, or by the pond's edge where it may be seen mirrored in the quiet waters.

The bumblebee is a regular visitor and the Baltimore butterfly is often found hovering nearby. Indeed this butterfly occurs only where the turtlehead grows and rarely wanders father than a hundred yards. Not that the butterfly visits the blossoms; It does so only on rare occasions. The reason it stays close is that the caterpillars feed on the leaves and do so almost exclusively. They feed on the plant in a communal web until autumn, then hibernate in the web, and in the spring continue their feeding, though now more solitary, until it is time to pupate. The emerging butterflies mate, the females lay their eggs on the leaves, and the cycle is repeated.

The flower of the turtlehead is more odd and striking than attractive but it deserves something more than a passing glance. The flower is not unlike a turtle's head. It is about an inch long with a calyx of five sepals and a corolla with two lips. The upper lip is broad and arched and notched at the apex. The lower lip is three-lobed at the apex and woolly-bearded in the throat. The flower has four dark and woolly stamens with woolly heart-shaped anthers and a single pistil that later develops into a many-seeded capsule.

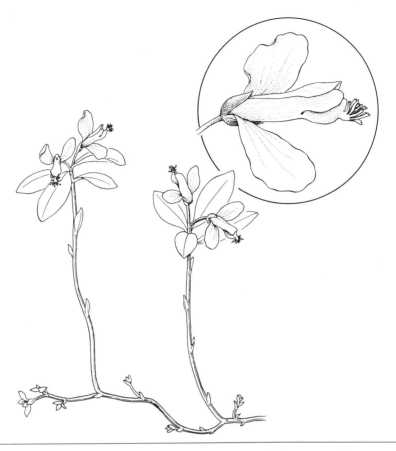

Fringed Polygala
Of butterfly beauty

I can still recall the time when I first saw the fringed polygala. I was walking along a country road and as I passed a stone wall my eye caught a bit of crimson and I wondered what butterfly had settled there. But on looking closer I saw that it was not a butterfly but a most dainty little flower that was almost hidden from view by its surrounding leaves.

The fringed polygala is common in damp rich woods but it is such a low growing plant that we really have to look for it. The flowering branches spring from prostrate stems and roots that are sometimes a foot long. They have a few broad ovate bright-green leaves crowded at the top—a few lower ones having been reduced to mere scales—that persist through the winter when they turn a bronze-red. The flowers are crimson or magenta—in rare instances they are white—of a rather peculiar shape suggesting an orchis. The outer envelope or *calyx* consists of five parts or *sepals* that are unequal in length. Two of them are broad, winglike, and colored like the three petals. These petals are united in a tube, with the lowest ending in a pouch containing the male and female organs, and beautifully fringed at the end. The last petal serves as a landing platform for bees that depress the pouch with their weight. This forces the rigid stamens and pistil out through a slit at the top of the pouch, thus coming in contact with the plant's visitors. Cross-fertilization is effected by the pollen carrying bee brushing against the exposed stigma of the next flower it visits. Honey bees and mining bees are the plant's chief visitors. In addition to the visible flowers, the fringed polygala also bears cleistogamous flowers that are hidden beneath the surface of the ground.

As William Hamilton Gibson wrote many years ago:

> The stroller in the moist May woods will well remember those mauve-winged blooms among the moss that seems to flutter in the breeze, like a brood of tiny purple butterflies with fringy tails, or in a sheltered nook appear to have settled in a swarm among the winter-green leaves. . . . It is one of our oldest and prettiest spring flowers; in its very singular shape quite suggesting an orchid, with its two spreading petals and deep lavender-colored tasselled sleeve. But indeed, it has long been laughing at us in that sleeve, as we have brought away its flowers from the woods.

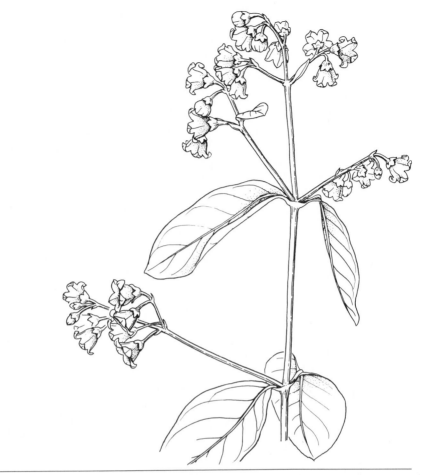

Spreading Dogbane
The inseparables

During the month of July it seems that we cannot stir far from the house without finding the spreading dogbane. This plant seems to be everywhere. It isn't, of course, but we do find it in the fields and thickets, beside roads, lanes, and stone walls, and even about our dooryard on occasion; Its delicate and beautiful white-pink and rose-veined bells suggest pink lilies of the valley. The little veins show where the nectar is and butterflies, bees, flies, and beetles come to feast. Some of these, however, pay for having trespassed on what is, in a sense, the butterflies' preserve. For the butterflies are best fitted to serve the dogbane. Many bees, flies, and other insects remain imprisoned in the flower's trap of horny teeth until death from starvation releases them.

The *spreading dogbane*—also called *honeybloom*, *bitterroot*, and *wild ipecac*—is an attractive and graceful plant. It usually grows in patches or colonies because of its extensive creeping horizontal rootstalks, from which new plants are sent up at intervals. It has a somewhat shrubby stem, one to three feet tall, that is generally reddish on the side exposed to the sun and opposite light blue-green ovate toothless leaves. The flowers are in small clusters at the ends of the branches and develop into twin follicles. The follicles are long, slender, curved, four inches long, and stuffed with many thin flat brown seeds, each with a tuft of long silky hairs that are reminiscent of milkweed seeds. As well they should be, for the spreading dogbane once belonged to the milkweed tribe and it has many of the same structural details as the milkweed, including the milky juice. There is further proof that the dogbane once belonged to the milkweed tribe, for the caterpillars of the monarch butterfly, though they feed almost exclusively on milkweeds, will at times include the dogbane in their dietary.

In July the dogbane beetle adopts the plant and they remain inseparable. I have never found the insect on any other plant. Resplendent in metallic green and red of an incomparable luster, the beetle is a beautiful insect and when they are on the foliage in great numbers the dogbane appears to be studded with jewels. If alarmed, to prevent capture, the beetle draws its legs up beneath its body and drops to the ground. There it becomes lost to view in the grass since its colors blend so well with the herbage.

The dogbane derives its name from the belief that it is poisonous to dogs. How much truth there is to this or whether dogs have ever been poisoned by it is not known. However horses, cattle, and sheep have died from eating its leaves.

Bloodroot
Of fleeting loveliness

In hidden copse and shaded thicket, along the woodland border, and on low hillsides the warm sunshine of April quickens into life the buds of the bloodroot. We can almost see them slowly emerge from the embrace of silvery-green leaf cloaks to expand into white-petaled golden-centered poppy-like flowers that offer us but a glimpse of the plant's fleeting loveliness. For on the morrow the delicate blossoms, unable to withstand the spring winds, will fall and vanish.

We might observe that the golden-orange anthers mature after the two-lobed stigma, which shrivels before the pollen is ripe, and that the outer stamens are somewhat shorter than the inner ones in an advanced flower. We might also observe that the stigma is prominent in a newly opened flower so that cross-pollination may be effected. The flower does not contain any nectar and attracts only those insects that gather pollen: the honey bees, bumblebees, smaller mining bees, bee-like flies, and flowerflies.

95

The bloodroot is a beautiful but fragile flower, one and a half inches broad, generally with eight brilliant white petals set on the end of a naked stalk. A single large round leaf, usually with seven irregular lobes, enfolds the bud and expands with it. Both the flower and leaf come from a thick rootstalk. Eventually the flower becomes an oblong dry pod holding many light yellow-brown seeds. Puncture the root or any other part of the plant and there flows a red-orange juice that stains whatever it touches. The Indians used it as a dye for baskets, clothing, and war paint, as well as an insect repellent. The bloodroot has an acrid and bitter taste and is said to be medicinal in quality. Thus F. Schuyler Mathews wrote in his *Familiar Flowers of Field and Garden:* "About the end of April, beside the road, on the brink of the river, in moist pastures, and beside the woodland brook, may be found the beautiful, broad white flowers of the plant which furnishes a famous specific for coughs and colds. Long before I became acquainted with the plant I had taken many drops of its orange-red blood on lump sugar."

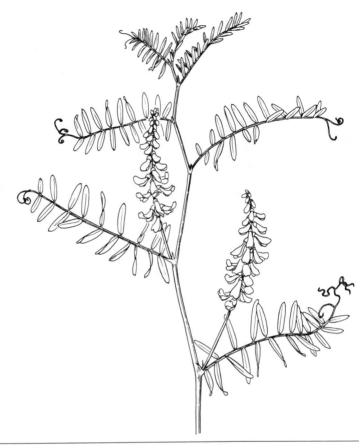

Cow Vetch

Patches of color that match the sky

When the June sun shines brightly and soft breezes blow over the landscape dotted with countless blossoms of many colors, the vetches, in fields and meadows, in thickets and along the roadside, and in waste places, mirror the sky with patches of blue. Or perhaps not exactly blue but rather purplish or violet: though whatever the color the bees reap a harvest.

There are about 150 species of vetches—some are annual and some are perennial, some are erect and others are climbing. But all have compound leaves with leaflets numbering between one and twelve pairs. Those in the climbing species have the end leaflet modified into a tendril for climbing purposes. One of the more common and more widely distributed of the vetches is the one generally known as the *cow vetch* or *blue vetch*. It is a graceful plant with a tough creeping rootstalk and tufted slender branches, two to four feet long. The branches climb by means of tendrils at the tips of each leaf stalk; the lance-shaped gray-green leaflets each terminate in a bristle-like point. The pea-like tubular flowers are violet-blue in color, the upper petal being lined with a deeper violet, and are fairly numerous in one-sided clusters that are sometimes as much as four inches long. They develop into pods of about an inch in length that contain five to eight small dark-brown globular seeds. Finally, the entire plant is covered with fine closely pressed hairs and is a soft olive-green in color.

The caterpillars of the common sulphur butterfly feed on the leaves and the Indians are said to have eaten the starchy seeds that, though smaller, resemble those of the cultivated pea.

On July 6, 1851 Thoreau wrote:

> *from the lane in front of Hawthorne's, I see dense beds of tufted vetch, for some time, taking the place of the grass in the low grounds, blue inclining in spots to lilac like the lupines. . . . It is affecting to see such an abundance of blueness in the grass. It affects the eyes, their celestial color. I see it afar, in masses on the hillsides near the meadow, much blue, laid on with heavy a hand.*

Harebell

Dancers in the wind

I saw the harebell for the first time along the grassy edge of a quiet pond. At the time I did not know that this seemingly delicate plant is as much at home in some inaccessible crevice of a precipice, among the rocks sprayed by the waters of a swiftly flowing mountain stream, or in a wind-swept upland meadow as in a sun kissed pondside.

The harebell is the bluebell of Scotland, the bluebell of literature, a cosmopolite found in Europe, Asia, and America. Despite its frail appearance it is a hardy plant capable of surviving the cold and storms of mountaintops more than five thousand feet above sea level. In the spring it shows a tuft of small sparingly toothed leaves that soon wither and disappear before the flowers begin to show and that are succeeded by a tall wiry stem, from six inches to three feet in height. This stem is supple and bends easily without damage before the strongest wind. It has narrow pointed pale olive-green leaves that offer little resistance

99

to moving air currents, however strong, and bright-blue or violet-blue nodding bell-shaped flowers, depending from thread-like stems. The calyx has five awl-shaped lobes, the corolla is five-lobed, the stamens are five in number, the anthers have a delicate lavender tint, and the prominent pistil is tipped with a three-lobed stigma that is green at first and white later.

But the flower of the harebell was not always like it is today; at some time in the past it welded its five petals together, first at the base, then farther and farther up its sides, until a solid bell-shaped structure resulted. This arrangement makes for more effective fertilization by insects since little of the pollen is lost through openings and since an insect visitor can enter the flower only where the stigma comes in contact with its pollen covered body. The colors of the harebell flower are attractive to our eyes and also appeal to insects such as the bees, butterflies, and bee like flies, though its chief visitor is the bumblebee. And we should also bear in mind that the drooping position of the flowers protects their pollen from rain or dew.

I have always had a special regard for the harebell since I first saw the dainty flowers along the grassy edge of the pond. Standing, I watched them dance in the slight breeze that flowed over the pond with what might almost be regarded as gleeful abandon. I have also watched them dance in stronger winds when it seemed as if they would be torn apart.

Wood Sorrel

The plant that goes to sleep

One of the daintiest, if not the daintiest, of all our woodland plants is the wood sorrel. But we must look for it in the cool deep woods where the sunlight penetrates feebly through the leafy branches to reveal a vista of fallen logs and moss covered boulders. Children used to know it as the *plant that goes to sleep at night,* for at nightfall its leaflets droop and fold together to reopen at sunrise. This provision apparently was designed by nature to protect the plant from cold by radiation.

The wood sorrel is a stemless perennial that grows from creeping root-stalks. It has compound leaves, each from the root and each composed of three light-green heart-shaped leaflets, and delicate pretty flowers nearly an inch broad, with five notched petals that are pinkish-white and striped with crimson, or white with crimson lines. Each of these flowers is on a long slender stalk that, like the leafy stems, arises from the rootstalk. The small mining bees and the flowerflies visit the blossoms to ensure cross-fertilization but the plant also has *cleistogamous flowers*—flowers that are fertilized in the bud without opening—that are also borne on small curved stems at the base of the plant. The wood sorrel has an almost worldwide distribution, being found in Europe, Asia, and northern Africa, as well as in America.

The early Italian painters, Fra Angelico and Sandro Botticelli, made use of the wood sorrel's chaste beauty in their paintings. John Ruskin wrote "Fra Angelico's use of the *Oxalis Acetosella* [wood sorrel] is as faithful in representation as touching in feeling. The triple leaf of the plant and white flower stained purple probably gave it strange typical interest among the Christian painters."

At one time the plant throughout Europe had the rather odd name of *Hallelujah* because it blossomed between Easter and Whitsuntide, the season of the year when the Psalms sung in the churches resounded with that word. The old English name of *cuckoo-bread* was once applied to the plant because it blossomed at the time when the call of the cuckoo was first heard in the land. The three-divided leaves of the wood sorrel are considered to have been the shamrock of the ancient Irish.

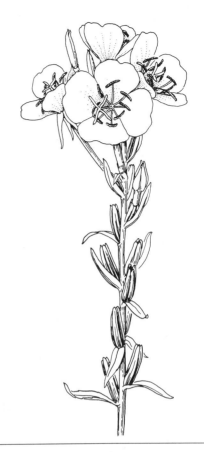

Evening Primrose

Miniature moons that gleam in the night

By day the evening primrose has little to commend it. When we see it by the roadside or in a thicket or fence corner, its wilted faded flowers and hairy capsules crowded among the willow-like leaves at the top give it a rather bedraggled appearance. But when the sun has set in the western sky and twilight begins to creep over the landscape, developing buds begin to open and pure-yellow lemon scented flowers appear and gleam like miniature moons after other flowers have melted into the deepening darkness. Bumblebees and honeybees may visit the flowers in the morning before they have had a chance to close but it is the night-flying moths that the plant depends upon for cross-pollination.

It is not without reason that the flowers are yellow, that their fragrance becomes stronger with the night, that the nectar wells are located in tubes so deep that none but the moths' long tongues can drain the last drop, or that the golden pollen is loosely connected by cobwebby threads on eight prominent and spreading stamens. The Isabella tiger moth is perhaps the plant's chief benefactor but there are others among them the spinx moths; when morning comes we may find a little rose-pink moth, its wings bordered with yellow, asleep in a wilted blossom. Since the flowers turn pink when faded the moth is safe from prying eyes. Later in the summer when enough seed has been set the evening primrose changes its habit and the flowers remain open all day. Cut open one of the brown seed capsules and you can see the small brown seeds neatly arranged in eight parallel rows.

> *A tuft of evening primroses*
> *O'er which the wind may hover till it dozes*
> *O'er which it might well take a pleasant sleep*
> *But that it is ever started by the leap*
> *Of buds into ripe flowers.*

This poem expresses the sentiment of the evening primrose well. It has a stout and somewhat hairy stem that is two to six feet or more in height. Its root leaves are lance-shaped, dark-green, and slightly toothed and its stem leaves are much smaller. Its flowers are in terminal clusters and easily recognized by their long calyx tube, which may be as much as two inches in length, and at the end of which is the flower.

The evening primrose is a native of our shores but was cultivated in English gardens in the early 1600's for its edible roots that are supposed to be wholesome and nutritious when boiled. In various parts of Europe the roots were used for food and the young shoots for salads. The herbalist Parkinson was the first to describe this night blooming flower from the new world and gave it the name of *primrose* because its scent reminded him of the wild primroses in English meadows.

The evening primrose is a biennial and hence during our winter walks we might see close against the ground the rosettes of year old plants, symmetrical complex stars from whose center, flower stalks will arise the coming summer.

Some years ago William Hamilton Gibson wrote:

> *Can we really claim to know our evening primrose? Night after night, for weeks, its pale blooms have opened, and shed abroad their sweet perfume in the darkness in every glen and by every roadside, and yet how few of us have ever stopped to witness that beautiful impatience of the swelling bud, the eager bursting of its bounds, and the magic unfolding of the crinkly yellow petals.*

Burdock

To make a bird's nest

I can remember that when I was a boy we used to toss the burs of the burdock at each other with mischievous glee, for they would cling to our clothing and at times we would be covered with them. The girls, not deigning to engage in such rowdy play, preferred to make birds' nests, dolls, and baskets out of them. The burs seem to be familiar to almost everyone as the plant is common along the roadside, in old fields and waste places, along fence rows, and about old dwellings; but if you have never looked closely at one, do so with a hand lens and you will see why they cling so tenaciously to our clothing as well as to the fur of animals. Each bur consists of a number of one-seeded fruits called achenes that are oblong, three-angled, and ribbed, with one end truncate and the other in the shape of a hook.

The burdock has an enormous root, often three inches thick, penetrating the ground straight down for a foot or more and then branching in all directions. It also has a much branched stem four to eight feet in height. The leaves are large, dull-green, and veiny; the lower ones are heart-shaped and often a foot long; the upper ones are ovate and woolly beneath. The globular flower heads, hooked bristling green burs with magenta or nearly white perfect tubular florets, are a standing invitation to butterflies, which delight in magenta, and to bees of various kinds. To appreciate its depth of coloring we should look at a flower head with a magnifying glass or hand lens. The flowers appear from July to October.

The seeds and roots of the burdock were once used in medicine and the leaves are said to have been cultivated as vegetables in Japan. In our own country the large tender leafstalks have been peeled and eaten raw, used as a salad, or cooked like asparagus, which it has been said to resemble in flavor.

Jewelweed

Like jewels from a lady's ear

With its orange-yellow flowers spotted with reddish-brown and hanging like jewels from a lady's ear, the jewelweed is a familiar plant in wet places. It grows beside streams, ponds, and in moist dells and is known to all of us who know the outdoors. It is a juicy-stemmed herb, two to four feet tall, with alternate thin pale coarsely toothed leaves and irregular perfect flowers that have three sepals and three petals. However, these sepals and petals are not easily distinguishable. One of the sepals is large and sac-shaped. Contracted into a slender incurved spur, it is admirably adapted to the long bill of the hummingbird but you have to examine the flower closely to see how well it serves its purpose. Of course insects visit the jewelweed too, particularly the long-tongued bumblebee.

But as if the lovely jewelweed did not have enough confidence in its visitors to depend upon them entirely to perpetuate the species, it also develops cleistogamous blossoms that never open but which ripen self-fertilized seeds.

And yet enough cross-pollinated seed is produced to prevent the species from becoming degenerate, something that often follows close inbreeding.

On a dewy morning or after a shower, visit the jewelweed where it grows along a woodland brook or in the moist ground by the edge of a pond and you will find the notched edges of the drooping leaves hung with dewdrops that sparkle like jewels in the sunshine. I doubt if you could find another name for the plant that would be more fitting. Still the jewelweed does have another name, *the touch-me-not.* The fruiting capsules into which the flowers eventually develop are overly sensitive to the touch when ripe; merely touch them and they will open with startling suddenness to expel their tiny seeds a distance of as much as four feet. You may well be frightened or startled at the unexpected volley from the miniature machine gun.

A technical explanation of the phenomenon is that the capsule breaks up into five spiral coiled valves that expel the seeds.

William Hamilton Gibson wrote some years ago:

The touch-me-not with its translucent, juicy stem and its queer little golden flowers with spotted throats—the 'jewel-weed' we used to call it. This is the dewy night's rarest treasure. It is indeed a jewel. Upon the approach of twilight each leaf droops as if wilted, and from the notches along its edge the crystal beads begin to grow, until its border is hung full with its gems. It is Aladdin's lantern that you set among a bed of these succulent green plants, for the spectacle is like a dream land.

Common Cinquefoil
or Five-Finger
A miniature yellow rose

Beginning in April, if we are observant, we will notice small yellow flowers beginning to appear in field and meadow, along the roadside, on the hillside, in the pasture, and also in waste places. As many in the past have done, we may mistake it for a yellow flowered strawberry and call it a wild strawberry. But a strawberry will never develop from the flower; instead, if all goes well, eventually there will appear a number of single seeded fruits called achenes.

We need only to glance at one of the little yellow flowers of the *cinquefoil* to observe its resemblance to the rose; indeed, under the magnification of the hand lens we could very well take it for a yellow rose. Compare it with any rose, wild or cultivated, and you will see that they have much in common: five sepals, five petals, and many stamens in multiples of five. There are some 300 species of cinquefoil found everywhere in the northern temperate and subarctic regions. Our most common species is the *five-finger*, a name alluding to the five leaflets that spread like the fingers of a hand.

It is a low spreading plant with silvery down-tufted stems that are six inches to two feet long. The deep-green shiny oblong leaflets are sharply toothed. The flowers are solitary and fertilized mostly by the flowerflies.

The name *cinquefoil* is derived from the two words *cinque,* meaning *five,* and *feuilles,* meaning *leaves,* and during the Middle Ages when almost any plant was regarded as having curative properties the cinquefoils were especially viewed as having healing virtues for almost any ailment. Pliny, for instance, wrote that cinquefoil, honey, and axle grease mixed together formed an efficacious ointment for scrofula, and Linnaeus named the genus of cinquefoils *Potentilla*—from the Latin *potens* or *powerful*—because of their reputation as powerful cure-alls.

Wild Strawberry

A delicacy of flavor

One of the more pleasant experiences of our rambles outdoors in the spring, whether in field or pasture, along the roadside, or even in some woodland, is suddenly to come upon the white flowers of the wild strawberry blossoming close to the ground. For not only are the leaves most attractive to the eye but the flowers also appeal to our sense of the aesthetic; the many orange stamens provide a delightful contrast to the white petals, especially when seen with a lens.

And later when the fruit has matured there is an even more delightful experience that awaits us, especially if we have never tasted one before, for the "berry" is fragrant and the most delicious of all our wild fruits. Indeed it has a flavor that the largest juiciest cultivated strawberry cannot provide. As someone once said: "I had rather have a pint of wild strawberries than a gallon of tame ones."

The wild strawberry is a low growing perennial that forms runners, with compound leaves of three leaflets that are rather broad, coarsely toothed, blunt tipped, and hairy. These are set on long stems that are covered with soft hairs and that come from the roots. The flowers appear in April, have five white petals, many orange-yellow stamens, and numerous pistils, and are borne on stems that are shorter than those of the leaves. They are followed by the scarlet fruit that ripens in June or July. It is in the much enlarged juicy fleshy receptacle that the true fruits—commonly called achenes or, incorrectly, seeds—are embedded.

And we may well pause and ask how the *strawberry* got its name. Some say that in early times it was named for the straw that was laid between the roots to keep the fruit clean. Others claim that in earliest Anglo-Saxon it was called *streowberie*—and later *straberry*—because of its peculiar straying suckers that lay as if strewn on the ground.

In his *Travels*, in June of 1776, William Barton wrote:

> ... We enjoyed a most enchanting view—a vast expanse of green meadows and strawberry fields, a meandering river gliding through, turfy knolls embellished with parterres of flowers and fruitful strawberry beds, flocks of turkeys strolling about them, herds of deer prancing in the meads or bounding over the hills, companies of young, innocent Cherokee virgins, some busy gathering the rich, fragrant fruit. Others, having already filled their baskets, lay reclined under the shade of floriferous and fragrant bowers ... disclosing their beauties to the fluttering breeze and bathing their limbs in the cool, fleeting streams whilst other parties, more gay and libertine, were yet collecting strawberries, or wantonly chasing their companions, tantalizing them, staining their lips and cheeks with the rich fruit. ...

Celandine

Of saffron juice

The American botanist, Gray, tells us that the generic name of the *celandine*, *Chelidonium*, meaning *a swallow*, was given to it because its flowers appear when the returning swallows are seen skimming over ponds and streams and freshly ploughed fields. But quaint old Gerarde wrote that it was not given its name "because it first springeth at the coming in of the swallowes, or dieth when they go away, for as we have said, it may be founde all the yeare, but because some holde opinion, that with this herbe the dams restore sight to their young ones, when their eies be put out."

Whatever the origin of the name may be, the celandine—a native of Europe—has found its way to our shores and we find it growing in roadsides, woodland borders, fields, waste places, and even in our own gardens and about our dooryards. It is a plant some twelve to thirty inches in height with deeply divided or cleft leaves. These are distinctly pale-bluish-green underneath and the terminal one is the largest. The celandine has small yellow flowers with two sepals, four petals, many yellow stamens, and a green style. These flowers occur in small stalked clusters. When bruised the plant exudes a yellow or orange juice with a disagreeable bitter acrid odor. Like that of the bloodroot, this juice stains whatever it comes in contact with. It was once considered a sure cure for warts, corns, pimples, and the like. The fruit is a smooth pod, one to two inches long, with smooth shining dark-brown seeds that have a white crest like a cock's comb on one side.

The celandine is not an unattractive plant; quite the contrary, it blossoms cheerily wherever it takes root. But there is little satisfaction in picking a flower that droops immediately, poppy fashion, or one whose juice stains whatever it touches.

White Baneberry

China eyes

I think most of us would regard with suspicion any wildflower that has as part of its name the word *bane*, for the dictionary defines that word to mean harmful or injurious: and so the white baneberry is, for its curious fruits are poisonous and children should be warned against placing them in their mouths.

It is a plant of cool moist shady woods with an erect stem that is one to two feet tall and leaves that are divided two or three times into sharply toothed and pointed, sometimes lobed, leaflets. The flowers that appear in May and June are small and white in terminal oblong clusters. The petals are very small and from four to ten in number, the stamens are white and numerous and longer than the petals, and the flowers include a single pistil with a broad stigma. They are followed by a cluster of shiny white berries, each with a dark purple spot, the stems of which are thick, fleshy, and usually red. These berries have been graphically compared to the china eyes once used in dolls and for generations they have also been known as *doll's eyes.* Needless to say, in the woods these fruit clusters are most conspicuous.

The white baneberry does not secrete any nectar and yet it is visited by the smaller bees for its pollen.

A related species, the red baneberry is similar in appearance to the white baneberry but may be recognized by its more ovoid cluster of feathery white flowers, its less sharply pointed leaves, and by its clusters of oval red berries. Like those of the white baneberry they are both conspicuous in the woods and also poisonous.

Poison Hemlock

Of ancient usage

It is a rather odd commentary on nature that a plant family that has given us the carrot, parsnip, parsley, celery, caraway, fennel, and coriander also could include some of our most poisonous plants as well: the spotted cowbane, water hemlock, and poison hemlock. The last is reputedly the plant from which a decoction was made that Socrates and various criminals of Athens were forced to drink—the so-called *cup of death.*

The poison hemlock is probably the most dangerous of all our wild-flowers because all parts of the plant are exceedingly poisonous. Domestic animals usually die from eating the leaves in spring, though sometimes they recover. Children have been killed by mistaking the seeds for fennel or caraway and adults have been fatally stricken by eating the leaves or roots thinking the leaves were those of the parsley and the roots were parsnips.

The poison hemlock is a native of Europe and Asia but has become naturalized in the United States, being rather common on waysides, in waste places, and about farm buildings. It is a smooth erect many branched hollow stemmed plant, from two to five feet tall, with dark-green leaves that are deeply dissected and toothed and that resemble those of the parsley. It has a stem which is often purple spotted, a white parsnip-like root, and tiny five-petaled white flowers in large open terminal clusters. The seeds are ovate, flat, grayish-brown when ripe, and prominently ribbed with a deep groove on the flattened surface. When bruised the entire plant gives off a *mousy* odor. It blooms from June through August.

Bees and wasps appear to be the most numerous of the plant's visitors. Indeed the poison hemlock appears to attract more of these insects than any other member of the carrot family.

Pokeweed

Red ink

In our rambles afield during the month of July we might not take much notice of a plant with white flowers and large leaves, but in September it is well nigh impossible for this same plant to escape our attention. Then its tall purple stems rise above their neighbors, its leaves appear as if stained with wine, and long clusters of rich dark berries weigh heavily from the branches. As Thoreau once wrote, its clusters "of berries of various hues, from green to dark purple, six or seven inches long, are gracefully drooping on all sides, offering repasts to the birds, and even the sepals from which the birds have picked the berries are a brilliant lake-red, with crimson, flame-like reflections, equal to any thing of the kind—all on fire with ripeness."

And if we pause a moment and watch the birds eating the fruit we are likely to see robins, flickers, downy woodpeckers, towhees, and rose-breasted grosbeaks among others. These will carry the undigested seeds far and wide. I have seen the birds become intoxicated from eating the berries.

The *pokeweed*—also known as the *pokeberry, pigeonberry,* and *inkberry*—is a handsome plant, albeit a dangerous one, for its root is very poisonous and children have suffered from eating its berries. Yet both have been used extensively in the preparation of certain drugs and as a household remedy for skin diseases and rheumatism. And if the young shoots are cooked thoroughly and the water is changed several times they make excellent greens or a substitute for asparagus. In some places the berries have been used with whiskey to make a so-called *port-wine* and, because of their dark juice, an ink; hence the plant is also known as the inkberry, as we have already mentioned.

The pokeweed is a four to ten foot tall plant that grows along fencerows, in thickets and waste places, as well as in our dooryards. It has a stout smooth usually red or purplish stem and oblong lance-shaped rather thick deep-green entire leaves that have an unpleasant odor when bruised. The flowers are white and occur in terminal clusters; the calyx is white with five rounded sepals that are petal-like, the petals being absent. Each blossom produces a juicy dark-purple berry.

The flowers are under special obligation to the small mining bees but other short-tongued bees, as well as flies, also serve as its benefactors. And when the insects are not flying the flowers are adapted to fertilize themselves.

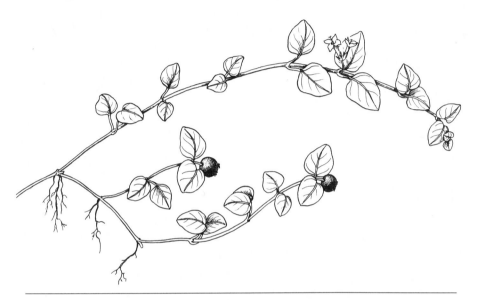

Partridge Vine
Of delicate fragrance

Whether it is in June when its little evergreen leaves are sprinkled with pairs of waxy cream-white, pink-tipped delicately-scented flowers or in autumn or winter when its coral red *berries* gleam in the shade of the woodland floor, the partridge berry, to my mind, is always one of the most glorious sights to be seen in the woods.

It is a little trailing vine, six to twelve inches long, with heart-shaped dark-green leaves, occasionally having white veins, on short stems and with two kinds of flowers. In some plants the stamens extend beyond the corolla and the pistil is shorter than the corolla tube while in others the stamens are short and the pistil extends beyond the corolla tube. This is a device to insure cross-pollination by insects such as the mining bees, though some of the smaller butterflies, for example, the clouded sulphur, the meadow fritillary, and the painted lady, are also effective pollinators.

The flowers grow in pairs—hence the name *twinflower*, as the plant is sometimes known—and are so united at the base that it takes two blossoms to form one *berry*. Or as the poet expressed it:

Made glad with springtime fancies pearly white
Two tender blossoms on a single stem
In their sweet coral fruitage close unite
As round head cut from a garnet red.

The bright red *berries*, which are actually drupes, persist on the vines all winter and are edible but rather tasteless. They are eaten by some game birds such as the bobwhite quail and ruffed grouse. The latter is sometimes known as the *partridge*. That is where the plant gets its name. But they are not of too much importance to wildlife even when the birds and various animals often have trouble finding enough to eat. It is said that the Indian women once made a tea from the leaves that was useful in childbirth.

Early Saxifrage

The rock breaker

Were we to explore a rocky woodland or a rocky hillside in early spring we would most likely find rosettes of fresh green leaves rooted in the clefts of the rocks. And were we to examine the rosettes carefully we would observe small finely haired balls in the center of the leafy tuffets. These would shortly expand into branching downy stems bearing many little white perfect star-like flowers, each with five sepals, five petals, ten yellow stamens, and two pistils.

The flowers are visited by the early bees and by such butterflies as the mourning cloak and tortoise shell and are succeeded by rather odd madder-purple two-beaked seed vessels. And why the downy stems? The hairs are sticky, thus guarding the flowers from unwanted pilferers—for example, the crawling ants—whose feet become ensnared in them.

This little plant that we find growing among the rocks and blooming among the first flowers of spring is known as the *early saxifrage;* The name comes from the Latin for *rock-breaker* and has been interpreted as meaning that the saxifrage grows in rocky crevices that it has broken open in order to gain a foothold. The Germans know it as the *Steinbrech* or *stonebreak*. In ancient times the plant was used to break down kidney stones.

In his *The Native Ferns and Flowers of the United States*, Thomas Meehan wrote:

> *None of the saxifrages seem to have excited poetic fire, nor have they entered in any way into the arts . . . Before it flowers it forms one of the most beautiful rosettes imaginable. For the central ornament in a piece of carving, it would furnish an admirable pattern. With the warm weather, the green of the leaves becomes prettily tinted with rose, and at this stage the plant is in nice condition for the artist, to whom these departing shades in the sunset of plant-life are always welcome.*

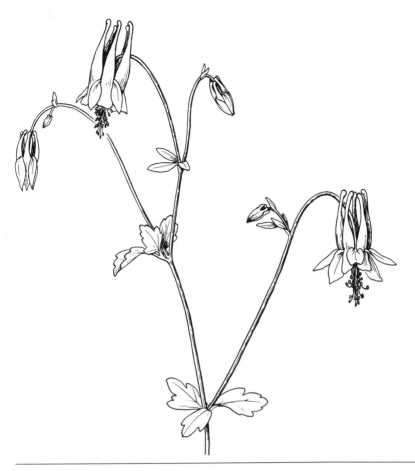

Wild Columbine

Of daring loveliness

Though considerably larger and more showy than the wild varieties, the cultivated columbines I have in my garden somehow lack the appeal of those I find
in the woods where their scarlet and yellow cornucopias dance in the breeze with
elfin charm. I think this is true with most flowers, at least with the wild ones, for
when I have transported them from the fields or woods to the garden many of
them do not seem to belong. There are some who will disagree with me, but I
much prefer to see most flowers in their natural surroundings. Of course, many
of them are garden escapes, but presumably all of them were originally wildings.

There is a sort of daring loveliness about our wild columbine which
seems to linger in our memory long after we have seen it on some rocky hillside
or on the border of a wooded glen. Paradoxically, it is a delicate but hardy plant
with a branching stem that is one to two feet tall and long-stemmed compound
leaves made up of three-lobed light-olive-green leaflets. The flower is most

unique and interesting. There are five petals, which are red on the outside and lined with yellow within. These petals are funnel-shaped and narrow into long erect very slender hollow spurs that are rounded at the tip and united below by the five ruddy yellow sepals. Between these sepals the straight spurs ascend, and the knobs at the end are filled with nectar. There are many stamens and five pistils, the latter developing into five long erect pods that are tipped with the slender styles.

The long spurs—they suggested to an imaginative Linnaeus the talons of an eagle; hence he named the group of columbines *aquila*—are an adaptation of the flower to the long-tongued insects. And perhaps, if we are fortunate while in contemplation of this favorite flower, we might suddenly see a ruby-throat appear and then as quickly sail away again after having emptied the five spurs of their nectar.

The name *columbine* is said to have been derived from *colomba*—a *dove*—because of the "resemblance of its nectaries to the heads of pigeons in a ring around a dish, a favorite device of ancient artists." But this derivation of its name is highly disputed.

We find many glimpses of the columbine in early English literature and Shakespeare refers to it quite frequently. Our native columbine was once sent as a gift from the Virginia colony to Tradescant—botanist to King Charles I—who introduced it to the Hampton Court gardens. Indeed, the columbine has, at various times, been suggested for our national American flower.

Emerson knew the columbine well for he wrote:

> . . . *A woodland walk*
> *A quest of river grapes, a mocking thrush*
> *A wild rose or rock-loving columbine*
> *Salve my worst wounds.*

And as a final note, in addition to the various insects that visit the columbine for its nectar or pollen, the columbine dusky wing has adopted the plant as a food plant for its caterpillars.

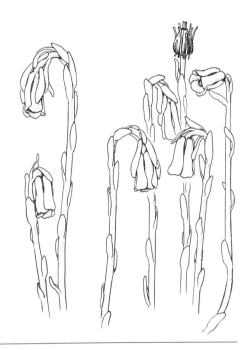

Indian Pipe
A company of wraiths

I still experience a thrill when I come upon a company of Indian pipes rising with ghostly grace from among the brown debris of the woodland floor. They are such unusual plants, being waxy, cold, clammy, and colorless in every part, that they almost seem to be visitors from another world. They are both parasites and saprophytes, obtaining their sustenance equally from the juices of living plants and from the decaying matter of dead ones. Among the shadows of the forest they are weirdly beautiful and decorative.

The stem of the Indian pipe, which is from three to eight inches tall, rises from a ball of matted rootlets and is thick, translucent white, and leafless, the leaves having given way in the dim remote past to scaly bracts. The flower is smooth, waxy, white—on rare occasions pink—oblong, bell-shaped and nodding. It is composed of four or five wedge-shaped petals, between eight and ten pale tan stamens, and a single pistil. As the ovary matures it becomes enlarged

127

and erect and eventually develops into an ovoid capsule. A mere glance at this odd plant would hardly suggest that it is a relative, on the one hand, of some of the showiest and loveliest flowers among our flora—the azaleas, laurels and rhododendrons—and on the other hand, of the modest but no less charming pipsissewa and wintergreen.

Pick the plant and it quickly turns black as if in protest of such unseemly conduct. Because of this it has been called *life in death* and the *corpse-plant*. The plant was once used by the Indians as an eye lotion and some of them believed it to have healing properties.

Blue Vervain

The herb of grace

For many of us the blue vervain has it greatest appeal when the snow lies on the ground, the sun shines brightly, and its dried stalks etch delicate shadows on the snow. As John Burroughs wrote, "they make a pretty etching upon the winter snow." Certainly its purple blossoms are too small to be attractive nor are the slender stalks appealing, though they branch upward like the arms of a candelabra. The reason is that they have buds at the top, flowers in the middle, and brown nutlets at the bottom, an arrangement that grates on our sense of the aesthetic. And the name of the plant is also misleading, for the flowers are not blue nor do they approach any semblance of blue. Flowers, however, were not designed for our enjoyment but to attract the insects, and many bumblebees, honey bees, and mining bees, as well as some of the smaller butterflies such as the checkered white, are usually seen about the blossoms, sometimes appearing to be asleep on the blossoming spikes.

In Shakespeare's time the vervain was believed to be a charm against witches and in ancient times it was used as a charm to bring lost love back. As Virgil wrote:

> *Bring forth water, and encircle all altars with a soft fillet*
> *Burn thereon oily vervain and male frankincense*
> *That I may try, by sacred magic spells*
> *To make my lover madly love.*

Undoubtedly the plant Virgil referred to was the *verbena*—the *herba sacra*—used, according to Pliny, in ancient Roman sacrifices. The early Christians accorded healing virtues to the vervain growing on Mount Calvary and the Druids counted it among their sacred plants. Later, witches, regarding it as an enchanter's plant, gathered it and used it as an ingredient in their brew to help them perform mischief with their incantations. However it also seemed to work against them for Drayton says of it, "gainst witchcraft much avayling." In more modern times the vervain has been regarded as an *herb of grace* and has been gathered for various ceremonies with the invocation of a blessing that began:

> *Hallowed be thou Vervain*
> *As thou growest on the ground*
> *For in the Mount of Calvary*
> *There thou was first found.*

The vervain has also been known as *Simpler's joy*, the Simplers being the gatherers of medicinal herbs, to whom no plant was more valuable.

The blue vervain, an attractive perennial of fields, meadows, thickets, and roadsides, has a tall erect stout four-sided grooved dull-green stem some three to seven feet tall, branching near the top. It also has short-stemmed leaves that are dark-green, oblong or lance-shaped, double-toothed, and finely rough haired. The small five-lobed tubular flowers occur on numerous spikes that branch upward like the arms of a candelabra. They are usually grouped in a small circlet about the stem, a green stretch of buds above and one of ripening fruits below. These flowers develop into small brown nutlets.

The flowers, which appear from June to September, have a five-toothed calyx, a five-lobed corolla that is unequally lobed, two pairs of stamens and a pistil, and we usually see bees, the plant's chief benefactors, clinging to the flowering spikes and seemingly asleep upon them.

Common Mallow
Wee tubs of cheese

Children of another day called its seed vessels *wee tubs of cheese* and ate them when green because they were then mucilaginous and sweet. Hence we know the plant today as *cheeses* but like other wildflowers it has other names too—the *common mallow*, the *running mallow*, the *dwarf mallow*, and the *round-leaved mallow*. The word mallow comes from the Greek word for a group of plants and means *soft*, and it was given to them either because of their soft downy leaves or because of the soothing properties of their roots. These have been used in cough syrups and for "internal irritations," as old medical books had it. Pliny even goes so far as to say that one spoonful of syrup from any one of the mallows would relieve anyone from all disease from that time on. And from the roots of the *marsh mallow*—a species that grows in the salt marshes—marshmallows were once made.

A native of Europe, the common mallow is an escape like so many other plant immigrants and today we find it in waste places everywhere as well as in our gardens and about our dooryards, where we consider it a weed. It has deep branching roots that seem to spread nearly as far beneath the ground as its creeping stems do above. The stems are six inches to nearly two feet in length, round, smooth, and branched at the base with round or kidney-shaped dark-green leaves that usually have five shallow scalloped-shaped lobes. The leaves are on long stalks. The flowers are pale-pink, veined with deeper pink, and are clustered in the leaf axils. The calyx is hairy, ovate, pointed, and has five lobes. There are five petals, which are notched at the tips. The stamens are united in a column around the style with the anthers at the summit and with very large white pollen grains that, when seen through a lens, look like pearls. And the flowers too, when viewed through a magnifying glass, bear a close resemblance to the hollyhocks; indeed we might almost say that they are miniature hollyhocks. The fruit is somewhat distinctive and consists of perhaps as many as fifteen round flat segments arranged in a ring that resembles a wheel of cheese.

Pythagoras valued the plant as a spinach; so did other Greeks and Romans as well. It is still cultivated as a potherb in Egypt and the tender shoots are eaten today as a salad in France and Italy.

Common Sunflower

Yellow heads looking toward the sky

Moore's well known lines,

> *As the sunflower turns on her god, when he sets*
> *The same look which she turn'd when he rose,*

have been seriously questioned and generally regarded as a poet's fancy. Yet it has been said that the head of the common sunflower does change its direction, to a certain extent, with the sun from east to west.

The sunflower we find growing in meadows, waste places, fence rows, and along the roadsides is the common sunflower—the sunflower of our gardens, where it sometimes grows as tall as ten feet with flower heads a foot or so in diameter. In the wild it commonly grows from three to six feet in height with flower heads from three to six inches in diameter. The disk florets are brown, purplish-brown, or purple and the ray flowers are bright-yellow.

The common sunflower—the state flower of Kansas—is said to be a native of the western states. It ranges from Minnesota to Idaho and south to Texas and California, and it is also an escape in the East. However, it is said to be a native of South America—of Mexico and Peru—because the Spanish conquistadors found it used there as a mystic and sacred symbol, in much the same manner as the Egyptians used the lotus in their sculpture. However that may be, when Champlain and Segur visited the Indians of Lake Huron's eastern shore about three hundred years ago they found them cultivating the plant; its stem provided them with textile fiber, its leaves fodder, its flowers a yellow dye, and its seeds food and a hair oil. Lewis and Clark related that when they were along the Missouri River in western Montana,

> . . . along the bottoms, which have a covering of high grass, we observe the sunflower blooming in great abundance. The Indians of the Missouri, more especially those who do not cultivate maize, make great use of the seed of this plant for bread, or in thickening of their soup. They first parch and then pound it between two stones, until it is reduced to a fine meal. Sometimes they add a portion of water, and drink it thus diluted; at other times they add a sufficient proportion of marrow-grease to reduce it to the consistency of common dough and eat it in that manner. This last composition we preferred to all the rest, and thought it at that time a very palatable dish.

The sunflower seems to be more appreciated in some countries in Europe than in the United States. There it is cultivated for its flowers, which yield a fine yellow dye, and for its seeds, which yield an oil used for cooking, burning, or for soapmaking. The oil cake makes an excellent food for cattle. In some places the seeds are roasted and used as a substitute for coffee, and in Russia the seeds are not only used for poultry food but are also ground into meal that is used in baking bread and cakes. In addition the various species of sunflowers serve as food plants for the caterpillars of the silvery checkerspot and the painted lady. And as everyone who has a bird feeder knows, sunflower seeds are avidly eaten by many of our songbirds.

> *Eagle of flowers! I see thee stand*
> *And on the sun's noon-glory gaze*
> *With eye like his, thy lids expand*
> *And fringe their disk with golden rays.*

There seems hardly any question why the *sunflower* should have been so named: from its great flower head with its encircling rays of gorgeous yellow petals. The common sunflower has a rough erect stem, usually from three to eight feet tall, that branches at the top. The leaves are three inches to a foot in length and are broadly oval or nearly triangular with rough stiff hairs. The flower heads are from three to six inches broad with many large bright-yellow sterile rays. The disk florets are tubular, five-lobed, dark-purple or brown, perfect, and fertile. These develop into large oblong achenes that are nearly smooth and grayish-brown with white marginal stripes.

Steeplebush

A spire reaching for the sky

As we ramble about the countryside during the summer months our attention is often attracted to the spires of the steeplebush as they reach for the sky. This is true also for the countless bees, flies, beetles, and other insects that seek the abundant pollen of the flowers, which bloom in spike-like clusters, either for themselves or for their progeny. Thus they become agents of cross-fertilization. Indeed, so many insects may be found about the blossoms that anyone interested in collecting them will find the plant a good hunting ground.

The steeplebush is a plant of moist meadows and swamps, of roadside ditches, old fields, and hillside pastures. It has an erect stem that is two to four feet tall. The bark is red and clothed in rusty wool that rubs off readily. It has long ovate leaves that are smooth and green above but covered on the lower surface with tawny or whitish wool. The flowers are tiny and colored a deep rose-pink or sometimes a reddish-purple. Each has five sepals and five petals, many stamens, and five to eight pistils, and they are crowded in dense terminal spike-like clusters that later develop into roundish pointed follicles that are woolly and filled with small brown seeds.

If we examine the steeplebush closely we may well ask why the lower surfaces of the leaves are so woolly. Doubtless they act as a protective absorbent to prevent the pores, or *stomata*, in the leaves from becoming clogged with the vapors that rise from the damp ground upon which the plant so often grows. Every plant, like every animal, must breathe. They must take in oxygen and give off carbon dioxide waste, a process known as *respiration*. They also must be able to get rid of any excess moisture taken in by the roots, a process called *transpiration*. All this is effected by the pores in the leaves and stems and were they to malfunction, were they to become clogged with dust, dirt, or the like, the plant would suffer and, in extreme cases, die.

Cardinal Flower

The nonpareil

Doubtless it was the early French Canadians who were so enamored of the beauty of the cardinal flower that they sent the plant to France as a specimen of what could be found in the wilds of the new world. There it may have been given its name by virtue of being the same color as the hat worn by a prince of the Roman church.

The deep red of the blossoms—a deeper red than that of the bird of the same name—almost seems to kindle into flame the moist thickets where we find it growing.

> *As if some wounded eagle's breast*
> *Slow throbbing o'er the plain*
> *Had left its airy path impressed*
> *In drops of scarlet rain.*

Not many insects visit the blossoms for their tongues are not long enough, but the hummingbird can reach the nectar. And we may well ask, why the hummingbird does not visit the cardinal's twin sister, the blue lobelia. The flowers are built based on similar plans, though the lobelia is slightly adapted for the bumblebee, which is a frequent visitor. Is it the color of the blossoms? If we study the habits of the ruby-throat we will find that its visits are confined chiefly to such flowers as the painted cup, oswego tea, coral honeysuckle, columbine, and the garden salvia, fuchsia, and phlox.

Who has not seen the cardinal flower in blossom along a brook, a meadow runnel, or even a roadside ditch? If it wanted to hide among the surrounding vegetation it could not do so any more than the scarlet tanager could conceal itself among the leafy branches of a tree. It is a stately flower of considerable beauty and is one of our own plants; it is not an importation from some distant place but a plant strictly indigenous to America.

It is a tall stiff plant, its stem is sometimes as much as four feet in height, with toothed dark-green oblong to lance-shaped leaves. The upper leaves are stemless. The flowers are in terminal clusters. They are tube-shaped and two-lipped; the upper lip is two-lobed and the lower is three-lobed. The stamens are united in a tube that extends beyond the corolla. The flowers are of a rich velvety color and appear from June to September. They are followed by a many-seeded pod.

In writing of the cardinal flower on August 13, 1842 Nathaniel Hawthorne had this to say:

> For the last two or three days, I have seen scattered stalks of the cardinal flower, the gorgeous scarlet of which it is a joy even to remember. The world is made brighter and summer by flowers of such a hue. Even perfume, which otherwise is the soul and spirit of a flower, may be spared when it arrays itself in this scarlet glory. It is a flower of thought and feeling, too; it seems to have its roots deep down in the hearts of those who gaze at it. Other bright flowers sometimes impress me as wanting sentiment, but it is not so with this.

Peppergrass

A spicy taste

Whenever I am afield I invariably place some of the seed pods of the pepper-grass between my teeth so that I may savor their spicy taste. That is, I do so if they are available, which is usually from June to October. These seeds, inciden-tally, have been used to season soups and stews, and the leaves of the plant are often used in salads or cooked as greens. And I might also add that the birds are fond of the seeds.

The peppergrass, which occurs in grain and clover fields, along road-sides, and in waste places almost everywhere, has a many-branched stem that is six inches to two feet tall; finger-like basal leaves with a few small lateral divi-sions or lobes; lance-shaped stem leaves that are toothed and small; and tiny white flowers, having four petals and only two stamens, that are arranged in elongated clusters. These flowers develop into rounded flatted pods that are slightly notched at the top and that contain two yellow-reddish seeds.

Water Lily

The water queen

Who has not seen, on a glorious summer morning, the water queen floating serenely on the quiet waters of a pond or in some shadowy pool, its golden centered chalice open to the sky. Its delicious fragrance beckons to bees and flowerflies and beetles and skippers who are on the wing, and who have admired, from afar, the beauty of this spotless and queenly blossom.

The words of Lucy Larcom speak of the water lily:

From the reek of the pond the lily
Has risen in raiment white
A spirit of air and water
A form of incarnate light
Yet except for the rooted stem
That steadies her diadem
Except for the earth she is nourished by
Could the soul of the lily have climbed to the sky.

Each radiant cup that rises with every undulating flow of the water is anchored to the bottom of the pond or pool by a long strong hollow stem, or *petiole*, that is designed to withstand the stress and pull of mud and water. The life of a blossom is about three days, opening in the morning and closing at night. Then the petiole begins to curve and coil and finally to pull the developing seed pod beneath the water where it ripens and drops the seeds to the bottom of the pond.

The leaves—roundish, leathery, thick, and purplish-red beneath and dark-green above—have floated since May. In June the buds begin to appear and gradually make their way to the surface on stems that adjust to the water's depth. Then when the summer days have grown long and warm they open into many petalled chalices, often five inches in diameter, with numerous yellow stamens. They are so perfect in form and so delicate in texture that we cannot help but admire their exquisite beauty.

Meadowsweet

Miniature apple blossoms in a cluster

If we are observant we will notice that, beginning in June, feathery spires will appear throughout the summer on the landscape in places along the roadsides, in rocky pastures, in waste places, in meadows and old fields, and on river banks. We know the plant as the *meadowsweet* but the name is something of a misnomer for the plant is not fragrant—or if it is, it is only slightly so.

> *And near the unfrequented roads*
> *By waysides scorched with barren heat*
> *In clouded pink or softer white*
> *She holds the summer's generous light*
> *Our native meadow-sweet.*

In spite of what Dora Read Goodale said of it, the meadowsweet seems to prefer hillside pastures where it can grow undisturbed by grazing animals, who dislike its astringent bitter taste, but we also find it growing in low moist ground, in meadows, and in old fields. Its stems are two to four feet tall with smooth reddish or purple-brown bark. They are simple or branching near the top and have a sort of wiry character. On these stems are set thin smooth dark-green leaves that are three times longer than they are broad and ovate and sharply toothed. The flowers, which resemble miniature apple blossoms are clustered in a beautiful pyramidal terminal spike. They are small—about a quarter of an inch wide—white or pale-pink, and have five sepals, five petals, five pistils and many prominent pink-red stamens. Unfortunately the blossoms open from the summit downward and as the summer advances the plume-like clusters begin to turn brown at the top. Small bees, flowerflies, and beetles are among the many visitors that come in great numbers seeking the accessible pollen and nectar. The latter is secreted in a conspicuous orange-colored disk. The fruit is a brown pod that remains on the plant after flowering and is thus a distinctive feature.

Boneset

A tonic of sorts

One hundred or more years ago you could have gone into almost any farmhouse and seen bunches of an herb hanging in the attic or shed, a grim warning of what would happen to anyone who might come down with a cold or a similar ailment. A brew made from the leaves had a most nauseous taste and children especially dreaded it, having to have it poured down their throats. It is said that the Indians were the first to discover its virtues. It seems that the decoction made from the leaves was especially adapted to cure a disease peculiar to the southern states known as *break bone fever*, or *dengue*. The early herb doctors also used the leaves to set bones by wrapping them around splints with bandages.

The boneset, a common plant we find growing in wet meadows, swamps, along the sides of streams and ditches, in wet woods, and along the roadsides, is a coarse stout herb that is three to six feet tall and branches at the top. It has light-green pointed finely scalloped leaves that are opposite and so closely joined that they appear as one leaf, perforated by the remarkably hairy plant stem. The flowers are tubular, perfect, small, and dull-white and occur in dense flat topped clusters. They furnish an abundance of nectar but butterflies do not seem to favor the plant, apparently preferring flowers of a deeper color. However beetles, bees, flies, and wasps find the flowers to their liking and crowd about them in large numbers.

Personally I have never tasted a brew made from the leaves of the boneset so I cannot describe its taste, but Alice Morse Earle wrote in her book, *Old Time Gardens,* that she had tasted it "many a time, and it has a clear, clean bitter taste, no stronger than any bitter beer or ale."

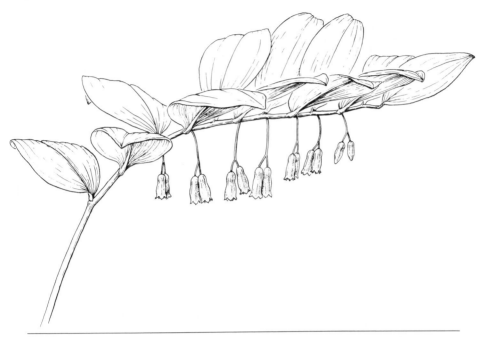

Solomon's Seal

With arching stems and pendulous flowers

If we were to dig up and examine the many jointed, thick rootstalk of the plant we know as *solomon's seal* we would find that it contains a number of scars, these large round scars having been formed by the death and separation of the base of the stout stalks of previous years. Hence we may determine the age of the plant by the number of scars on its root, in the same way that we determine the age of a tree by the number of rings in its trunk. As these scars resemble the impression of a seal upon wax it occurred to someone of a fanciful mind that they had a certain likeness to the seal of the great Hebrew king, and so the plant came to be known by the name it bears today.

We find the solomon's seal in woods, thickets, and shady banks where its graceful leafy stems and its pendulous blossoms mark it as one of the most decorative features of our spring woods. It grows to a height of between one and three feet. Its light green leaves are oblong-ovate, smooth and stalkless, and arranged alternately on the stem. Its tubular bell-shaped whitish or yellowish-green perfect flowers droop in pairs beneath them. The fruit, at first a green berry with a whitish bloom, eventually turns blue-black and is reminiscent of a small Concord grape.

During the spring the tender plant is said to be an excellent vegetable when boiled and served like asparagus. It is said that the American Indians ate the starchy root and Francis Parkman tells us that it was also used as food by the half-starved French colonists who had settled on our shores.

As is so often the case, the origin of the name *solomon's seal* is in dispute. One view is that the name was given to it because of its age-old use as a balm for sealing or closing fresh wounds. Gerarde wrote that "Dioscorides [first century Greek physician and author] writeth, That the roots are excellent good for to seal up green wounds; whereupon it was called Sigillum Salomonis of the singular virtue that it hath in sealing up or healing up wounds, broken bones and such like."

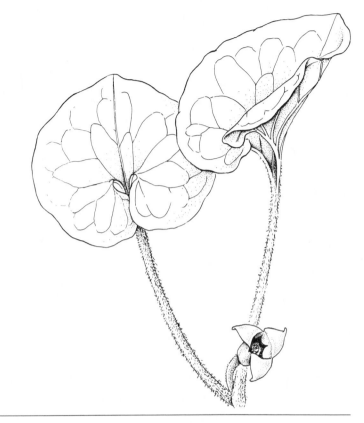

Wild Ginger

A picture of shyness

Probably the best way to find the wild ginger is to look for its heart-shaped or kidney-shaped leaves, which may be from three to six inches in width, though it is not always easy to locate them. Though their shape is distinctive, they blend in well with the litter of the woodland floor. As for the flower itself, it is even more difficult to find it because it opens close to the ground, is partially concealed by the leaves rising above it, and its sober color frequently resembles the leaf mold just beneath it.

The wild ginger is a somewhat curious plant with an aromatic rootstalk—once used dried and pulverized as a remedy for whooping cough and as a substitute for ginger—and two long-stemmed deep-green veiny soft woolly leaves. There is but a single flower on a short nodding stem from the bases of the leafstalks and near the surface of the ground. It lacks any petals; the calyx is bell-shaped with three-pointed brownish or madder-purple lobes closely united to the ovary or solid seed vessel. It persists until the seeds contained within a fleshy, roundish capsule have ripened. Then the capsule bursts irregularly, discharging the many seeds.

The wild ginger is an early spring flower of rich woods and hillsides. The low position of the flower and the frequent visits of fungus gnats and early flesh flies suggest that these insects are the ones most actively engaged in cross-pollination.

We may wander about the spring woods at will, quite oblivious perhaps that at our very feet a rather unpretentious flower—a very picture of shyness—prefers to hide among its fuzzy leaves rather than risk comparison with others of more brilliance.

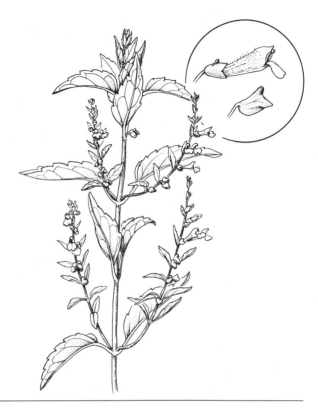

Mad-Dog Skullcap
A cure for hydrophobia

We have come a long ways since the time when old herb doctors professed to cure hydrophobia with a plant we know as the mad-dog skullcap. History does not tell us what happened to those bitten by mad dogs and treated with the plant but we can easily surmise that they could not have lived for very long.

The mad-dog skullcap is a bitter perennial herb common in damp and shady places. It has a square smooth leafy branched stem eight inches to two feet in height. The leaves are opposite, oblong to lance-shaped, coarse-toothed, and occur on slender stems. The flowers are small—about a quarter of an inch long—light or pale-purple, and are borne in succession along the delicate stems that terminate the branches or develop from between the leaf stem and plant stem. The calyx is two-lipped; the upper lip has a helmet-like appendage that children used to delight in pressing open when in fruit to reveal the four tiny seeds attached at the base. The corolla is also two-lipped; the lower one is three-lobed and spreading, the middle one is larger than the side ones and forms a convenient platform for the bees to alight upon. The stamens in the roof of a newly opened blossom dust the backs of visitors who explore the nectary. The flowers appear during July and August and eventually develop into nutlets.

Chickweed

A distinctive reputation

To use an old cliche, appearances are often deceiving. It certainly holds true in the case of the common chickweed, in spite of its frail appearance probably the hardiest and most persistent plant in the world.

The chickweed is found throughout the world—its range even nears the Arctic Circle—and it grows almost anywhere: in fields, meadows, roadsides, woods, waste places, lawns, and gardens. And we can find it blossoming almost any time of the year except in severely cold weather, but even then its green stems with buds, flowers, and seeds usually may be seen in some sheltered place. Its long flowering season is one reason why it can be found almost anywhere throughout the world. Another is that it can readily adjust to changing conditions and will quickly take possession of any unoccupied place. A third is that it can fertilize itself when it is too cold for insect pollinators to be abroad so it produces abundant seed even in the winter.

Every gardener knows the chickweed—the familiar weak stemmed low lying weed. Its stems have a single line of hairs down the side, and small ovate-pointed light-green leaves, and small white flowers with five petals that are almost cut in two and five green sepals that are much longer than the petals. And every gardener knows that if left alone the chickweed would eventually usurp every inch of garden soil.

During the warmer parts of the year the flowers are visited by the small bees, flies, and even the thrips and eventually develop into small round pods that are eaten by the wild birds and sold in stores for caged birds. The plant can be eaten in a salad and when properly prepared makes a splendid potherb.

In spite of its lowly estate as a weed the chickweed deserves its distinctive reputation for being a most unusual and successful plant.

It hardly seems necessary to add that the *chickweed* got its name because both the seeds and young foliage are relished by birds and chickens; and apparently they always have been for the ancient Latin name for it was *Morsus gallinae*, which when translated means *a morsel or bite for hens*. In 1597 Gerarde wrote in his *Herbal:* "Little birds in cages, especially Linnets, are refreshed with the lesser Chickweed when they loath their meate."

Some years ago, in *Sharp Eyes*, William Hamilton Gibson wrote:

Even in midwinter, if you know its haunt in some sunny nook, you may dig away the snow, and pick its white, starry blossoms, larger and fuller now than those of summer. I recall a beautiful episode from one of my winter walks long ago. . . . I was skirting the borders of a swamp where every hollow between mound and tussock was roofed with thin, glassy ice left high and dry by the receding of the water beneath . . . one portion of the clear crystal roof disclosed a lush growth of the chickweed beneath, its starry blossoms rivalling the surrounding snow in whiteness. A mimic conservatory—no not a mimic, rather say the model, the "coldframe" which nursed its winter blossoms eons before the modern infringement of the florist was conceived of. . . .

Mullein

Sentinels of the pasture

It is said that the Roman soldiers dipped the stalks of the mullein in grease for use as torches, and I believe that the leaves are still used as wicks in some places. The early colonists filled their stockings with the leaves of the plant to keep themselves warm and the Indians lined their mocassins with them for the same purpose. A tea from the leaves has been made as a remedy for the pulmonary complaints of both men and beasts alike, the so-called *mullein tea* being highly esteemed by country people. It appears to have been so highly efficacious with cattle that it earned the name of *bullocks' lungwort*. A tea made from both the flowers and roots has been used to treat various ailments and the leaves have sometimes been applied to the skin as a remedy against sunburn and other skin inflammations.

In spite of being called the *American velvet plant*, the mullein was probably brought to our shores by the early colonists. Sometimes as tall as seven feet and at home in old fields, pastures, and waste places, the mullein is a conspicuous feature of the landscape with its yellow flowers an inch or so across and its leaves covered with velvet hairs. When grouped together and seen from a distance, silhouetted against the sky they appear as sentinels to warn of danger should their homestead be threatened. A mere glance at the mullein will show that in addition to the few small pointed leaves that are seated on the stout erect stem there is also a rosette of basal leaves. These are thick, pale-green, and densely woolly with branched and interlacing hairs. Grazing animals will not touch these felt-like hairs but hibernating insects find them a safe winter shelter. But we may well ask why it has such woolly leaves; it is simply to help the exquisite rosettes formed by the year old plants to endure through the winter so that they can send up a flower stalk the second spring.

The flowers have a yellow corolla of five unequal rounded lobes, a very woolly calyx with five pointed lobes, and five stamens. The three upper stamens are bearded, shorter, and have smaller anthers than the longer, lower ones. These flowers appear from June to September—on long dense spikes—and open only for a day. They are succeeded by others on an ever-lengthening spike. The older ones quickly produce capsules filled with many brown seeds and it is then that we may see the goldfinches congregating to feed on them. Hummingbirds have been seen collecting the hairs of the plant for lining their nests.

In *Travels into North America*, Peter Kalm wrote that "The Swedes here tie the leaves round their feet and arms, when they have the ague. Some of them prepared a tea from the leaves for dysentery. A Swede likewise told me that a decoction of the roots was injected into the wounds of cattle when afflicted with worms."

Virgin's Bower

With feathery tails

Gerarde named the plant because he thought it was "fit for the bower of a virgin." And so we have the *virgin's bower*—also known as the *wild clematis*—whose fleecy white clusters may be seen everywhere throughout the eastern half of the country during the summer months of July and August. It is a handsome trailing vine that drapes itself over the roadside shrubbery, over the vegetation of the woodland border, or even over a fence or wall. The wild clematis—named for the Greek word meaning a *climbing or slender vine*—does not climb by means of tendrils but by the leaf petioles or leaf stalks that fasten themselves about twigs and branches in a kind of sailor's knot. Darwin made some interesting experiments regarding the movements of the young shoots. Thus he found that "one revolved, describing a broad oval, in five hours, thirty minutes; and another in six hours, twelve minutes; they follow the course of the sun." Then to show how sensitive the young plants are he continued "I may mention that I just

157

touched the undersides of two with a little water color which, when dry, formed an excessively thin and minute crust; but this sufficed in twenty-four hours to cause both to bend downwards."

The stem of the virgin's bower is slightly woody and its opposite dark-green leaves are divided into three coarsely toothed leaflets. The flowers are about an inch across, are white and greenish, and occur in loose clusters from the axils. They are of two kinds, staminate and pistillate, usually on different, but sometimes on the same, plants. They lack petals but have four or five petal-like sepals and many stamens and pistils. The staminate flowers have white plumy stamens—those in the very center are pale-yellow—and four greenish-white sepals. The pistillate flowers have a group of carpels giving them a green center. They are visited by the bees, the bee-like flies, and the brilliantly colored flowerflies. After the flowers have become fertilized the styles begin to grow and become long hairy tails attached to the seed vessels. Therefore by autumn the flower clusters have become gray feathery masses that are more noticeable than when they were in blossom. They look so much like an *old man's beard* the plant is sometimes known by that name.

Beggar-Ticks
Unwanted travellers

If you don't know the beggar-ticks all you need to do is walk in the woods on some autumn day, and before you have gone very far you will most likely have made its acquaintance. For in all probability your clothing will have become covered with numerous small two-pronged barbed seed vessels that cling most tenaciously not only to clothing but also to the fur of animals. And thus they obtain free transportation to distant places.

The *beggar-ticks*—also called *stick-tight, devil's bootjack, pitchforks,* and *stick-seed,* popular names that suggest the plant's character—grow in moist soil, swamps, ditches, and meadows and is not a particularly prepossessing plant. It has a smooth erect branched reddish stem that may be anywhere from two to nine feet tall. The leaves are opposite and usually smooth. The lower ones are generally five-lobed with long-pointed terminal segments; the upper ones are three-parted or sometimes lance-shaped and sharply toothed. It has rayless bristly flower heads. The disk florets are tubular, orange-yellow, perfect, and fertile. The calyx of each floret is converted into a barbed implement for grappling animal fur and our clothing.

"How surely the desmodium [tick trefoil] growing on some cliff-side, or the bidens [beggar-ticks] on the edge of a pool, prophesy the coming of the traveller, brute or human, that will transport their seeds on his coat." So wrote Thoreau. The flowers of the beggar-ticks, incidentally, appear from July to October.

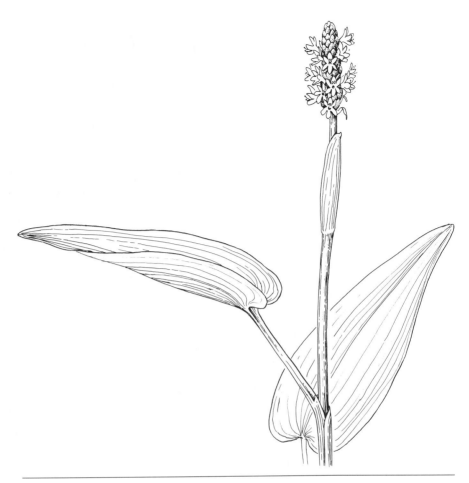

Pickerel Weed

A grace of habit

At one time, so it is said, someone saw the pickerel lay its eggs among the leaves of the *pickerel weed* and that is how the plant received its name. But the pickerel also lays its eggs among the sedges, arums, wild rice, and other water plants. Of greater importance perhaps, the pickerel weed, at home in the shallows of pond and stream, suggests to many people long summer days when trout, pickerel, and other fish swim slowly among the weeds that line the water's edge. They suggest days when turtles and frogs view us with wondering eye, when dragonflies dart swiftly through the air, when whirligig beetles play on the water's surface, and when bees, flies, and other insects congregate about the flowers that give color to the shoreline.

When in blossom the showy flower spike of the pickerel weed, crowded with ephemeral violet-blue flowers above the rich glossy spathe, invests this water-loving plant with a grace of habit and unique charm. Each flower—

marked with a distinct yellow-green spot—lasts only a day but is followed by a succession of blossoms on the gradually lengthening spike so that the plant blossoms, beginning in June, well into fall. The flower cup is funnel-shaped and divided into six parts. The upper three divisions are united and the lower three are spread apart. Three of the six stamens are long and protruding. The other three are short and often abortive. And the blue anthers are placed in such a way that it is impossible for an insect to enter the flower without brushing against them. The pickerel weed is a tall plant that grows to a height of four feet. It has thick triangular heart- or arrow-shaped leaves that extend above the water from the root. There is only one leaf on the flower stalk. Deer frequently visit the pond shores to feed on the plants.

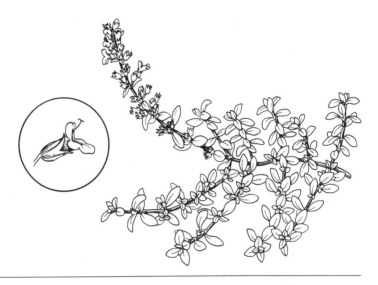

Thyme

A classic plant

I know a bank where the wild thyme blows
Where oxlips and the nodding violet grows
Quite over-canopied with luscious woodbine
With sweet musk-roses, and with eglantine.

So Shakespeare wrote in *A Midsummer Night's Dream.*

Many of us are acquainted with thyme—as well as with other herbs such as sage and marjoram—having cultivated it in our gardens. Thyme—an erect woody perennial with a strong mint-like odor—was highly prized by the Romans as a seasoning for various kinds of dishes. Ovid, Pliny, and Vergil all speak of it in relation to bees. The honey made from the nectar obtained from the small purplish flowers apparently has a pungent and aromatic flavor.

Thyme is said to have been one of the three plants used in making the

Virgin Mary's bed and it also appears to have been used as an incense in Greek temples. The Greeks found the honey much to their liking and regarded the plant as denoting graceful elegance and as an emblem of activity. "To smell of thyme" was high praise indeed, and given only to those with a faultless life style.

Our creeping thyme is a much branched low slender plant forming dense tufts from one root. It has small ovate leaves that are strongly veined and small purplish flowers that are crowded at the ends of the branches. The calyx is two-lipped and the corolla is slightly two-lipped. The flowers have two stamens and one pistil with a two-lobed style. We find this classic little plant, an emigrant from Europe, blossoming during July and August in old fields and similar places.

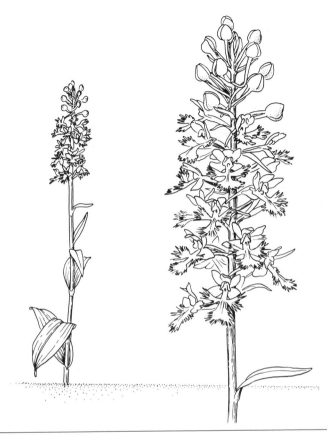

Purple-Fringed Orchis

The most striking of its clan

Perhaps no member of our flora has a more queenly appearance or is richer of hue than the one we know as the large purple-fringed orchis. We find it blossoming from June to August in wet meadows and cool rich woods. It grows twelve to thirty-six inches in height with oval or lance-shaped leaves. The bases of the leaves clasp the stem. The plant has fragrant purplish-violet flowers in a spike that is sometimes twelve inches long. The upper sepal and two lateral petals are erect. The lateral sepals are ovate and spreading. The lip is deeply three-parted, fringed, and prolonged into a long, thread-like spur. A glance at the spur would suggest that only a moth with a long tongue could reach the nectar secreted at the base of the thread-like passage. But butterflies are attracted by the conspicuous color and we often see them hovering about the blossoms, both the butterflies and moths having their heads and eyes decorated by the pear-shaped pollen masses.

Thoreau wrote:

> Find the great fringed orchis out apparently two or three days, two are almost fully out, two or three only budded; a large spike of peculiarly delicate, pale purple flowers growing in the luxuriant and shady swamp, amid hellebores, ferns, golden seneccio, etc. . . . The village belle never sees this more delicate belle of the swamp . . . A beauty reared in the shade of a convent, who has never strayed beyond the convent-bell. Only the skunk or owl, or other inhabitant of the swamp, beholds it.

Gill-Over-the-Ground

Making merry

At one time in Europe the aromatic leaves of a little creeping plant we know as *gill-over-the-ground* were used in fermenting beer or home-brewed ale that was then known as gill ale. Gill, it is said, was derived from the old French word *guiller,* meaning *to ferment or make merry.* That is where it gets its popular name. It is also said that the poor in England once made a tea from its leaves and perhaps they still do. Gerarde wrote that the plant was at one time highly prized as a domestic medicine: "boiled in mutton-broth it helpeth weake and akeing backs." It is a familiar weed about our houses and in towns and villages and seems almost domesticated; indeed we are not averse to having it about the house or garden for it strikes a welcome note in early spring with its small blue-violet flowers. And as its leaves remain green all winter there is always a bit of cheer, though the landscape may remain brown and sere.

The gill-over-the-ground—also known as *ground ivy*—is a prostrate creeping plant with slender stems and many small ascending branches. The stems sometimes grow twelve or more inches in length and root at the joints, having thus an easy way of forming new plants. The leaves are deep-green, kidney-shaped or heart-shaped, scalloped-toothed and they have slender stems. The flowers are pale purple, spotted with deeper purple, and occur in small axillary clusters. The corolla is about half an inch long, its upper lip with two lobes and the lower with three. The two upper stamens are nearly twice the length of the lower and rise against the upper lip. The tube is more than twice the length of the five-lobed hairy calyx. The fruit consists of four small brown nutlets.

Mrs. Willam Starr Dana wrote in *How to Know the Wild Flowers,*

> *As the pleasant aroma of its leaves suggests this little plant is closely allied to the catnip. Its common title of gill-over-the-ground appeals to one who is sufficiently without interest in pastureland (for it is obnoxious to cattle) to appreciate the pleasant fashion in which this little immigrant has made itself at home here, brightening the earth with such a generous profusion of blossoms every May.*

Peppermint, Spearmint
Clusters of bell-shaped flowers

The mint family consists of a great many plants, some 3000 species, mostly aromatic herbs. They are worldwide in distribution and found under a great variety of climatic and soil conditions. Superficially they all resemble each other and are somewhat difficult to identify as species but all have the family characters of a square stem and opposite simple leaves that are covered with tiny glands containing a strong-scented volatile oil of a peppery nature. The flowers are perfect, usually small, and tubular and have the corolla entire or with a two-lobed upper lip and a three-lobed lower lip. Hence the name of the family is *Labiatae*, from the Latin meaning *lips*. The calyx is regular or two-lipped and usually five-toothed or five-parted, the stamens are four in number, and the ovary is deeply four-lobed with the style arising from the center. The flowers have a two-lobed stigma. The fruit consists of four one-seeded bony nutlets.

Most of us have eaten peppermint candy and are familiar with its taste, but few would likely recognize the plant from the characteristic taste of the confection is in part derived since it grows along brooksides and ditches and in wet places. It is a perennial that spreads by creeping roots and that has a purplish stem eighteen to thirty-six inches in length. The leaves are two to three inches long, wrinkled, veiny, and toothed, and the purplish-pink blossoms occur in narrow loose disconnected terminal spikes and often on a long stem proceeding from between the plant stem and leaf stem. No one should have any difficulty in identifying the peppermint—all one needs to do is to chew the leaves—their intensely pungent aromatic taste resembles that of pepper and is unmistakable. One will also discover that the taste is accompanied by a peculiar sensation of coldness.

It has been said that in the Middle Ages spearmint was used as a charm against the bite of serpents, scorpions, and mad dogs. Of more serviceable use, it was employed in the making of cheese, incorporated with pennyroyal in puddings, and boiled with green peas. The latter is a custom that still prevails in England. Today both peppermint and spearmint are cultivated commercially for their essential oil, which is used in flavoring extracts, in confectioneries, in medicines, and in the case of peppermint in the manufacture of the cordial, creme de menthe. Many of us grow both the peppermint and spearmint in our gardens, using the leaves for seasoning. Spearmint is often served with vinegar as a sauce for roast lamb and sprigs of the plant are often used in making the seductive and intoxicating drink known as *mint julep* and in mint jelly.

Both the peppermint and spearmint are immigrants from Europe and Asia and both are escapes. Like the peppermint, the spearmint is also a perennial found growing from creeping rootstalks in wet places and along roadsides. It has a stem one to two feet in height and leaves two to three inches in length that are wrinkled, veiny, and coarsely toothed. Its small pale purple, bluish, or whitish flowers are clustered in whorls and form terminal interrupted spikes. Both peppermint and spearmint blossom during July and August and are visited by various flies, bees, and wasps.

We have a single native mint of our own. It is found in wet places and is more or less hairy all over with leaves that taper conspicuously from the center towards both ends. Lilac-white or white flowers are clustered in circles around the plant stem. It is said that the Maine Indians roasted the leaves before a fire and ate them with salt in the belief that they were nourishing.

Wild Indigo

For use as a dye

One of the most curious plants we are likely to find on our rambles abroad is the wild indigo. It has the unusual habit of turning black when it withers and then it looks as if it has been charred by fire. We find it blossoming from June to August in sandy soil everywhere. It is a smooth and slender plant, two to four feet in height, and it has a bushy luxuriance when growing in favorable situations. Its deep gray-green compound leaves, composed of three leaflets, are wedge-shaped and have a slight bloom. The flowers are small, pea-like, pure yellow, and in elongated terminal clusters. The calyx is four- or five-toothed, the corolla is formed of five oblong petals, and the keel encloses ten incurved stamens and one pistil. The flowers are visited by bumblebees, flowerflies, the leaf-cutter bee, and the mining bees of the genus *Halictus*. The latter are probably the most efficient agents of cross-pollination. The caterpillars of many butterflies, including the frosted elfin, the eastern-tailed blue, and the wild indigo dusky wing, feed on the leaves.

The young shoots are tender and in a way resemble asparagus; as a matter of fact there are places where they are gathered and used as a substitute for this green. It is said that the plant has also been used as a homeopathic remedy for typhoid fever. The plant received its name because some related species produce an inferior dye.

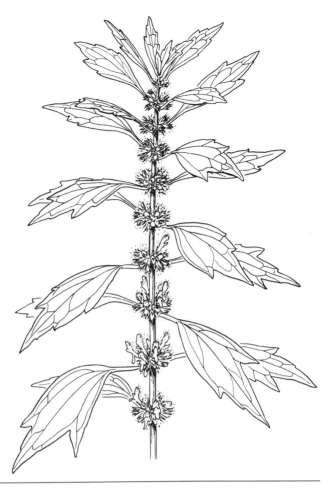

Motherwort

A social weed

John Burroughs once wrote: "one is tempted to say that the most human plants, after all, are the weeds. How they cling to man and follow him around the world, and spring up wherever he sets foot! How they crowd around his barns and dwellings, and throng his garden, and jostle and override each other in their strife to be near him!" Some of them become so familiar and domestic—and harmless besides—that we come to regard them with real affection. For instance, we have come to regard the motherwort as a sort of social weed, one rarely found far from human habitations.

It is a perpendicular growing decorative herb with a stout square stem that is two to five feet tall. Its dark-green leaves are finely and roughly haired. The lower ones are rounded and have palmate lobes. The higher ones become three-lobed and near the top often lance-shaped. They all have slender stems. The flowers—pink, pale purple, or white—are crowded in axillary whorls. The curving upper lip of the corolla is bearded inside. The lower lip is three-lobed and dotted purple. The flowers have four stamens and ascend against the upper lip. The green calyx has five thorn-like points that become hard and rigid, later containing four small brown three-angled nutlets. These have a blunt or truncate apex tipped with fine short bristly hairs.

The motherwort—a perennial immigrant from Europe but now an escape and common everywhere: about human habitations and barnyards, on roadsides, and in waste places and vacant city lots—blooms from June to August. It was once used by the herb doctors as a stimulant and for menstrual disorders; hence its common name of *mother*.

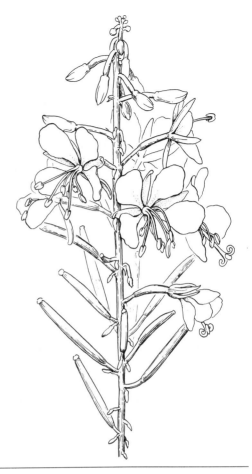

Fireweed

The phoenix of the flowers

In our rambles, if we ever want to find the fireweed all we need to do is to find a recently burned out area and we could be reasonably sure of finding it growing there. For the fireweed—like the phoenix—has a predilection for rising from the ashes. In such a place the spikes of the beautiful brilliant magenta flowers, on stems as large as eight feet in height, soon appear to cover the ugliness of the blackened ground as if nature abhored the unsightly devastation and had selected the fireweed to correct the situation. To be sure, other plants have also earned the name of fireweed but none so quickly beautifies an area recently scarred by fire as the *fireweed*, also known as the *great* or *spiked willow-herb*.

It is a tall plant with a stem that is somewhat woody, rather stout, erect, and usually reddish. Its alternate narrow lance-shaped leaves are olive-green, white ribbed, and without teeth or nearly so, and they resemble those of the willow. The flowers are purple, magenta, pink, or sometimes white; they are very showy and occur in terminal clusters. Each has four broad and conspicuous petals, eight stamens, and a prominent pistil. The flowers appear from June to September and, beginning at the bottom of the long spike or cluster, open in slow succession upward throughout the summer. They leave behind slender velvety purple-tinged gracefully curved pods that split lengthwise in September and send adrift white silky tufts attached to seeds that will someday perhaps beautify some distant waste. Invariably on a winter walk we will meet almost perfect rosettes made by the young plants.

The fireweed is a tall handsome plant found growing not only in burnt areas but also in low meadows and recently cleared woodlands. Pine woods, which are subject to frequent fires, are often alive with masses of the purple or pink flowers.

Thoreau wrote some years ago,

> I overtook the Indian at the edge of some burnt land, which extended three or four miles at least . . . an exceedingly wild and desolate region. Judging by the weeds and sprouts, it appeared to have been burnt about two years before. It was covered with charred trunks, either prostrate or standing, which crocked our clothes and hands. . . . and there were great fields of fireweed on all sides, the most extensive I ever saw, which presented great mass of pink.

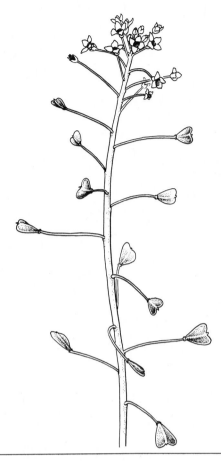

Shepherd's Purse

Little purses

Those of us who follow the byways of nature know the shepherd's purse well—its peculiar triangular seed pods are supposed to resemble the purse once carried by the shepherds—for it is a common and abundant wildflower that may be found growing along the roadsides and in fields and waste places. Indeed we may even find it in our gardens and on our lawns and about our dooryards.

It is a slender little plant, an importation from Europe, with small white flowers in a long loose cluster. These flowers are followed by the triangular and notched pods. Look closely at the plant and observe that one stem does service for all the flowers and that not one of them occurs at the tip for to do so would be to put a stop to its upward growth. Note also that the flowers, though individually small, are not entirely inconspicuous. This is because they are clustered together so that collectively they attract those insects, such as the flowerflies and houseflies, that aid in pollination. This is something that they might not succeed in doing were they arranged separately on the stem. And if the flies should fail then the long stamens standing on a level with the stigma are well calculated to self-pollinate the flowers.

This is the reason the shepherd's purse has been able to march around the world and compete successfully with other plants. Observe that as summer passes into autumn the plant continues to blossom until frost covers the ground. And even during the winter, when snow blankets the landscape, it will flower in sheltered and secluded nooks. By thus extending its flowering season far beyond that of any native flower it avoids the fierce competition for insect trade that it would otherwise have to contend with were it to flower during a shorter period. Noting the places where it is found growing, we find that it is not a proud plant and it will take root wherever it may. It is not choosy but is easily satisfied with unoccupied waste land and other localities where other plants refuse to grow. Is it any wonder that the shepherd's purse has been eminently successful?

The shepherd's purse is extremely variable but usually it has a rather deep taproot with many slender rootlets and a slender and branching stem six to twenty inches in height. The root leaves are deeply cut and form a rosette, the stem leaves are small, lance-shaped, and indistinctly toothed, and the flowers have six stamens and four petals that are arranged in the form of a cross. This is a distinguishing feature of all cruciferous plants.

White Clover

A ubiquitous flower

Unlike the red clover, its relative, the white clover is attended by bees in general since these are the insects that regularly effect cross-fertilization. We find this ubiquitous flower in fields, open wastelands, grassy roadsides, and cultivated places, as well as on our lawns. Its creeping branches send up solitary round heads of white or pinkish flowers on erect leafless stems. The heart-shaped leaflets are marked less distinctly with a triangle. As with the red clover each flower head is formed of numerous little florets, each one concealing nectar in a tube so deep that small insects cannot reach it. And once a floret has been fertilized it closes over its seed vessel, gradually withers and turns brown, and then hangs downward, thus giving notice to the next bee that comes along as to which florets still contain nectar and which do not. This also hides the developing seed pod from those insects whose young might feed on it and thus nullify the good work of the bees. Hence we may find many clover plants with some florets still open, waiting for a visit from some benefactor, while other florets are busily engaged in developing their seeds. By the end of the flowering season, which extends from May to October, all the florets are usually bent down and around the stem in a brown and crumpled mass.

But however well or successfully the clover plant guards its seeds from injury or destruction, it is unable to protect its leaves. These are a favorite food of grazing cattle and of the caterpillars of many butterflies, for example the common sulphur, the sleepy orange, the little sulphur, the northern cloudy wing, and the eastern-tailed blue. Incidentally, it is said that honey made from a field of clover is most delicious.

Yellow Rocket

Patches of yellow in the neighboring field

Some morning—perhaps as early as April—you may look out your window at the adjoining field and see it studded with patches of yellow. Or if you do not have such a view perhaps on your way to work you may pass a field similarly touched with nature's paintbrush.

As a rule the early spring flowers are small, shy, and seemingly delicate little plants and may be found more by accident than by painstaking search. There are exceptions, for example the *yellow rocket* or *winter cress*. It sends a dozen or more sturdy stems, at least a foot in height, upward from a single root crown. Each bears a cluster of brilliant yellow flowers that are frequently visited by the bees and handsome flowerflies. This is the plant that brightens fields and meadows and the banks of neglected runlets in early April when it gives color to a landscape that has not yet felt nature's artistry.

The yellow rocket is a member of the mustard clan but may be distinguished from all the other mustards by the large tufts of lyrate root-leaves. These are dark-green, thick, smooth, and shining, with heart-shaped terminal lobes. They occur in one to four lateral pairs along the midribs. When they first appear from beneath the winter snows these glossy green rosettes are quite conspicuous and may be used in salads or cooked as a potherb.

The flowering stalks are one to two feet in height and have sessile or clasping leaves. The flowers are in open clusters and are sweet-scented. They have four petals that form a cross, six stamens, and they later develop into erect seed pods—*siliques*—about an inch long with a short beak.

Both sheep and cattle feed with a greedy appetite on the winter cress. At times the planting of it as a forage has been advocated but its weedy habits and its pattern of never *staying put* have discouraged such attempts.

Field Sorrel
Of sour taste

In the northeastern states during the summer months the American copper, a small bright metallic coppery butterfly, may be seen flying about with careless abandon in city parks and village yards, as well as in the more open fields and woodlands. The caterpillars of this species feed on the field sorrel and the butterfly is often seen stopping to lay her eggs on the leaves and stems. The coppery-red color of the butterfly blends so well with the rusty-red of the blossoms that sometimes the butterfly is not noticeable on the plant until it moves its wings or suddenly takes to flight.

The field sorrel is a common plant—often a troublesome weed—from Europe. We find it in fields, meadows, pastures, roadsides, and waste places. Its extensively creeping branched yellowish rootstalk has tufts of feeding rootlets every few inches. Its stems are slender and erect—or almost so—and between three inches and a little more than a foot in height. The leaves are halberd-shaped on long petioles. The basal leaves have auricles, while the stem leaves usually do not. They are light-green and filled with an acid juice that gives them an unpleasant taste. The flowers are small and inconspicuous, reddish or greenish, and in clusters up to one half the length of the stem. The male and female flowers are on separate plants; the male is conspicuously yellow because of the pollen loaded anthers and the female has reddish calyx lobes and feathery crimson stigmas. The flowers blossom from June to October and when growing in pure stands are showy enough to attract the bees and the smaller butterflies. The seed-like fruit, which is a shiny golden-brown, is eaten by ground-feeding songbirds, and the leaves, even whole plants at times, are eaten by rabbits and deer.

Sweet Clover

Like new-mown hay

Once occupying a place among sweet herbs because its leaves are fragrant when dried—they have the fragrance of new mown hay when crushed—the *sweet clover* or *white melilot* is today considered a weed and an escape to the fields, roadsides, and waste places. I do not know why it is called a *clover; melilot* is a better name. Its generic name is *Melilotus*—Greek for *honey* and *lotus* in allusion to the fragrance of its foliage and its similarity to the genus, *Lotus.*

There is also a yellow melilot which is similar to the white species except for the color of its blossoms. Both sweet clovers are natives of Central Asia but came to us from the Mediterranean countries where they had been grown for centuries as forage and honey plants. They are considered weeds only when they grow in places where they are not wanted but useful plants otherwise for they have many good qualities. One is that they are *soil renovators.* Their large and deeply penetrating roots break up the soil; they mellow, aerate, and drain it;

and on their roots they bear many tubercles in which live the beneficient, nitrogen converting bacteria that transform the nitrogen of the air into nitrates and other soil enriching substances. They are also highly valued as honey plants.

The two sweet clovers are much alike and grow in the same places; indeed they are often seen growing together. Both have an erect round slender stem that is three to six feet or more in height with many spreading branches; compound leaves of three leaflets that are lance-shaped and toothed; and very small pea-like blossoms set in a long cylindrical spike-like cluster rising in the leaf axils. The flowers eventually develop into small ovoid pods. The seeds of both plants have a vanilla-like fragrance when crushed. The flowers of the sweet clover are said to have been used in flavoring Gruyère cheese, snuff, and smoking tobacco and as a camphor when packed with furs and woolens to preserve them against the ravages of moths.

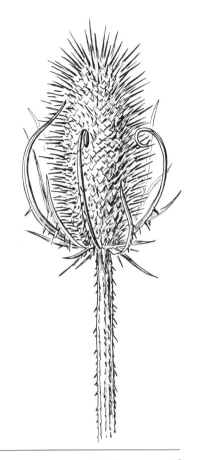

Teasel

Gypsy combs

At one time they were called *gypsy combs*—the dried flower heads of a wild-flower we know as the *teasel*—because they were used by the gypsy women to comb their hair. The dried heads had no equal in raising a nap on woolen cloth and so after the heads had withered the stems were cut to about eight inches in length, stripped of prickles to provide a handle, and dried. The natural tool was used to raise the nap on or to tease woolen cloth. Hence the common name of the plant.

The teasel is a unique plant in many ways. It is an immigrant from Europe found in pastures, roadsides, fence rows, old fields, and waste places. Its stout erect stem, three to six feet tall, is beset with spines and rises from a stout taproot often more than a foot long and with numerous rootlets. The root leaves of the previous year's growth are in broad and flat rosettes. They are lance-shaped and scallop-toothed. The stem leaves are opposite and lance-shaped. The rigid midrib is spiny on the lower surface and the bases of the leaves grow together to form small cups in which rain and dew collect; hence the generic name of *Dipsacus*, which is from the Greek *dipsa* meaning *thirst*. Sometimes the upper surfaces are covered with prickles—a somewhat curious feature for the prickles usually grow out of the veins.

The flowers, which bloom from July to September, are small, lilac or pinkish-purple, tubular, four-lobed, and fragrant and are clustered in large dense solitary heads, sometimes nearly four inches long and two inches thick. They are protected by long upcurving spiny bracts and are situated on long spiny stems that are both terminal and axillary.

Because of the stiff spines that radiate from the flower cluster the bumblebees can reach the florets only with their heads. Thus they cannot pollinize them by crawling over them as they do in other flowers.

The rain and dew that collects in the little cups was at one time considered by the country people to be a sure cure for warts. The little insects that often drowned in them were believed to afford nourishment to the plant.

Indian Cucumber

In the guise of a spider

It is said that the Indians relished the white thick succulent horizontal tuberous Indian cucumber root, which is said to resemble our garden cucumber in taste and smell. That is how it got its popular name, though its generic name, *Medeola,* is reputed to have been derived from the name of the sorceress, *Medea,* because it was supposed to have medicinal virtues.

It is a characteristic woodland plant, occurring in moist woods and thickets, well adapted to subdued sunlight, and interesting in both flower and fruit. Its single unbranched stem, one to two and a half feet in height, is covered with fine wool when it first appears in the spring. This wool later drops off. The plant has two whorls of leaves: a lower whorl of five to nine large thin oblong taper-pointed leaves about midway up the stem and an upper whorl of three to five small oval pointed leaves. The perfect flowers are inconspicuous and greenish-yellow but accented by the terra cotta color of the six stamens and the three long recurved terra-brown stigmas. The tip of the pistil is divided in three. The three sepals and three petals are also recurved. The entire flower reminds one of a spider. The flowers are set in a loose cluster on fine curving stems that sometimes bend down below the leaves and in September they are replaced by two or three purple-black berries. At this time the leaves take on rich tints and the Indian cucumber root becomes a truly beautiful plant, one that all of us should see if at all possible.

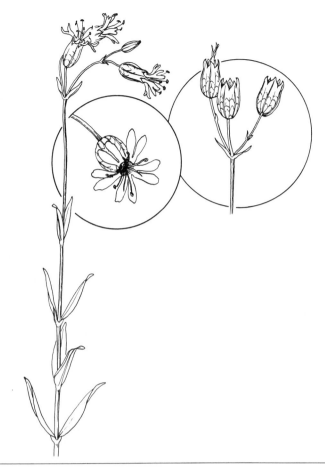

Bladder Campion

Like a miniature citrus melon

We might do well to give the bladder campion more than a passing glance, for its greatly inflated, pale green, and beautifully veined flower cup is not unlike a miniature citrus melon. Its white flowers gleam in the darkness and guide the moths that are seduced by the strong perfume that scents the night air.

The bladder campion—a delicately beautiful plant, albeit a pernicious weed—is a perennial species of Europe that has been naturalized in America. Here it may be found growing in fields, along roadsides, in meadows, and in waste places. Its stems are thickly tufted, pale-green with a white bloom, and smooth and grow from six inches to two feet in height. Its leaves are deep-green, oblong, and pointed. The upper ones often meet around the stem; the lower ones are usually finger-shaped and narrow to margined petioles. Its flowers are white and droop in loose open clusters. They have a pale-green and inflated calyx, a corolla of five deeply cut petals, and ten long stamens that are tipped with brown anthers.

Like some other night-blooming plants, the bladder campion has adapted itself to the night-flying moths. From June to August they are in constant attendance. Sometimes when morning comes the blossoms may remain open and bumblebees gladly avail themselves of whatever nectar remains in the deep cups. To ensure cross-fertilization some of the flowers have stamens only, some have a pistil only, and still others have both organs. When both are present they mature at different times.

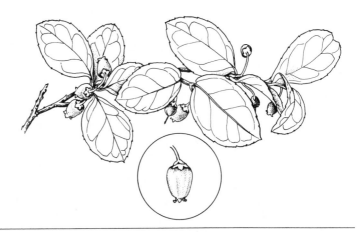

Wintergreen

Youngsters

Where cornel arch their cool
Dark bough o'er beds of wintergreen.

So wrote Bryant, but he did not know his plants too well. The wintergreen occurs more commonly in the vicinity of evergreens than near dogwoods.

All of us who know the woodlands are familiar with the shrubby plant that creeps upon or beneath the surface of the ground. Its erect branches—three to six inches tall—are terminated by the clusters of evergreen leaves. The older ones are dark-green, the younger are yellow-green. All are glossy and leathery, oval to oblong, finely saw-edged, and very aromatic. Children used to delight in chewing these tender yellow-green leaves in June when they first appear and at one time rural New Englanders called them *youngsters*. The older leaves may be eaten too but they are tougher and less agreeable. In many parts of the country a pleasing tea is made by steeping the leaves in boiling water. Hence the wintergreen is also known as mountain tea and teaberry. An extract is also used to flavor teas, candies, medicines, and chewing gum.

The flowers are white, waxy, vase-shaped, and nodding and grow from the axils of the leaves. The corolla is rounded, bell-shaped, and five-toothed; the calyx is five-parted and persistent and there are ten stamens. The anther sacs open by a pore at the top. The fruit is actually a capsule but is enclosed by the calyx, which thickens and turns fleshy, so that it appears as a globular red berry that has a pleasing spicy aromatic flavor. These vivid-red *berries* persist throughout the winter and find great favor with deer and bears and with such birds as the bob white and grouse. These birds will often plunge beneath the snow for such delicious fare.

That the wintergreen has 25 common names is evidence that it is one of the best known of our wild plants.

Canada Thistle
A vile pest

The American botanist, Asa Gray, called the Canada thistle "a vile pest," and in 1896 all but three of the states had laws making it an offense for anyone to mature and scatter its seeds. All this was because of its jointed horizontal rootstalks that are practically impossible to eradicate. They are round and slender—like tough white whipcords—and lie so deep in the ground that they are always sure to have moisture. Moreover they creep in every direction and send up new plants at frequent intervals. They defy all attempts to remove them.

The *Canada thistle*—so named because it came to us from Europe through Canada—is a common plant in pastures, fields, meadows, roadsides, and waste places. It has an erect slender grooved woody stem that is one to four feet tall and dull gray-green whitish ribbed leaves that are three to six inches long. These leaves are deeply cut, wavy-edged, and have hard white needle-like spines pointing in all directions. The small lilac, pale-magenta, or, on rare occasions, white flowers are in terminal or axillary clusters and contain about a hundred florets that are abundantly filled with nectar. They are fragrant and attract not only bees and butterflies but also flies, wasps, and beetles. They blossom from June to October.

Blue-Eyed Grass
Only for a day

If the blue-eyed grass had occurred in the Middle East we might well assume that it was the flower so graphically described in the passage in the Epistle of James:

> *For the sun is no sooner risen with a burning heat*
> *But it withered the grass*
> *And the flower thereof falleth*
> *And the grace of the fashion of it perisheth.*

Only for a day—and that day must be a bright one—will the blue-eyed grass open its flowers.

We find the blue-eyed grass blossoming from May to July in fields and moist meadows. It is a grass-like little plant that is four to twelve inches tall with stiff pale blue-green linear leaves and dainty violet-blue perfect flowers. The perianth is six parted; the divisions are blunt and tipped with a thorn-like point. The center of the flower is beautifully marked with a six-pointed white star accented with bright golden-yellow, each one of the star points penetrating the deeper violet-blue of the petal-like divisions. For that reason the plant has also been called the *blue star*. Bees and flowerflies are constant visitors. Following cross-pollination the flowers develop into dull-brown or purple-tinged sphere-shaped capsules. What it lacks in size the blue-eyed grass makes up in quantity and on any sunny spring morning almost any meadow will be punctuated by tufts of ultramarine-blue.

Lady's Thumb
A feminine imprint

During the summer months we should find, without much difficulty, a somewhat unique plant growing along the roadside, in damp waste places, and in cultivated ground. It is unique in that it has a singular mark in the center of each leaf that has a biblical connotation. For as the story goes, Joseph once injured his hand while working in his carpenter's shop. Mary wanted to make a healing poultice with this plant but

> she could not find it at her need
> and so she pinched it for a weed.

Ever since the leaves have borne the imprint of her thumb—hence its name.

The *lady's thumb* blossoms from June to October. It has nearly smooth stems six inches to two feet in height that are often red or purplish at the base. Its erect but sometimes spreading lance-shaped leaves are smooth or have fine hair along the edges, are pointed at both ends, and have a fairly large spot in the middle. The sheathing stipules at their base are fringed with short bristles. The small pink or purplish flowers occur in numerous erect oblong or cylindrical spikes a half-inch to two inches long. The calyx has four or five obtuse lobes. The flowers also usually have six stamens and a two- or three-part style. The fruit is seed-like, three-angled, and glossy-black.

Jamestown Weed
The white man's plant

When the settlers returned to the deserted foundations of Jamestown in 1609 Captain John Smith reported the presence of a weed that is now known variously as the *Jamestown weed, Jimson weed,* or *thorn apple.* In time it came to be so completely associated with the settlement at Jamestown that it became known by that name. However the Indians gradually learned to call it the *white man's plant.*

Asiatic in origin but of worldwide distribution, carried everywhere by the gypsies and a favorite medicine plant of theirs for ages, it is a plant of waste places, fields, barnyards, vacant city lots, and rubbish heaps. It grows three to five feet tall with, when young, a smooth green stout slightly hairy stem that branches by forking. It has large leaves that are rather thin and egg-shaped in outline. The edges are irregularly wavy-toothed or angled. The leaves have large veins, stout petioles, and a rank odor. The white trumpet-shaped flowers are solitary on short stems. The corolla is sometimes four inches long. The five-lobed mouth of the trumpet flares to a width of about two inches. The light green calyx, less than half the length of the corolla, has five sharp-pointed lobes. The five stamens are inserted a little below the middle of the corolla tube.

The flowers open late in the afternoon to welcome the sphinx moths whose tongues are long enough to seek the nectar. However, mischievous bees, flies, and beetles often manage to squeeze into the flowers as they begin to un-fold—not for the nectar but for the pollen that they sometimes remove entirely before the moths arrive. The flowers later develop into a dense prickly egg-shaped capsule with seeds that contain a powerful narcotic poison.

The Jamestown weed is a dangerously poisonous plant. In the past children have eaten the unripe seed pods with disastrous results and hence should be warned against them. Cattle, horses, and sheep have also been poisoned by eating the leaves. Susceptible persons may suffer a dermatitis simply by touching the leaves or flowers and should avoid doing so.

In 1705 Robert Beverly wrote in his *History of the Present State of Virginia*:

> this being an early plant, was gathered very young for a boiled salad, by some of the soldiers sent thither to quell the rebellion of Bacon (1676) and some of them ate plentifully of it, the effect of which was a very pleasant comedy, for they turned natural fools upon it for several days; one would blow up a feather in the air; another would dart straws at it with much fury; and another, stark naked, was sitting in a corner like a monkey grinning and making mows (grimaces) at them; a fourth would fondly kiss and paw his companions, and sneer in their faces, with a countenance more antic than any in a Dutch droll. In this frantic condition they were confined, lest they should, in the folly, destroy themselves—though it was observed that all their actions were full of innocence and good nature. Indeed, they were not very cleanly. A thousand such simple tricks they played, and after eleven days returned to themselves again, not remembering anything that had passed.

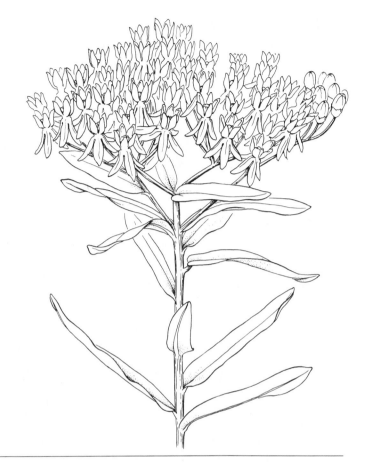

Butterfly Weed

The butterfly flower

If we transplant a few tufts of the butterfly flower or butterfly weed—whose intensely brilliant clusters set fields and pastures, hills and roadsides, ablaze with color during the summer months—into our own garden we may well give it an air of distinction and splendor.

Few flowers attract so many butterflies as the butterfly flower and hence it is well named. On any summer's day we may see various swallowtails—the tiger, the spicebush, the black, or parsnip—approach the brilliant clusters, hover about them, then alight, sip, and fly away. We may see many others as well—the white cabbage, the pearl crescent, the regal fritillary, the common sulphur, the bronze copper, the coral hair-streak—too numerous to mention except to say that here is a butterfly flower if ever there was one. And the reason is quite obvious; here is a flower that is well adapted to the butterflies, with their long limbs and long tongues.

The butterfly flower has an erect somewhat rough stem that is one to two feet tall, narrowly oblong and lance-shaped stemless light-olive-green leaves, and brilliant light-orange or orange-yellow flowers in erect flat-topped clusters at the ends of the branches. The five lower segments of the corolla are reflexed and the crown above it has five small spreading hoods, each having within it a slender incurving horn. There are five stamens that are inserted on the base of the corolla and the filaments form a tube that incloses the pistil, the anthers being adherent to the stigma. The flowers develop into twin follicles that are three to five inches long, covered with gray-hair, and pointed at both ends. The seeds are flat, margined, and brown and have a tuft of long silk hairs. They can be planted in the home garden if so desired.

The Indians used the tuberous root of the butterfly flower for various maladies, particularly as a cure for pleurisy. Hence the plant is also known as the *pleurisy root*. They also used the flowers as a dye and for food.

Dr. Charles Millspaugh wrote in *American Medicinal Plants,* published in 1887:

> *The pleurisy-root has received more attention as a medicine than any other species of this genus, having been regarded, almost since the discovery of this country, as a subtonic, diaphoretic, alterative, expectorant, diuretic, laxative, escharotic, carminative, anti-spasmodic, antipluritic, stomachic, astringent, anti-rheumatic, anti-sphilitic, and what not.*
>
> *For if any of our native plants add more to the beauty of the midsummer landscape than . . . the gorgeous butterfly-weed, whose vivid flowers flame from dry sandy meadows with such luxuriance of growth as to seem almost tropical. Even in the tropics one hardly sees anything more brilliant. . . .*

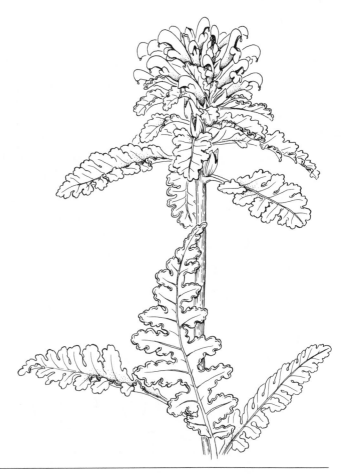

Wood Betony
An undeserved reputation

Years ago farmers believed that their cattle and sheep would become infested with lice from eating the leaves of a plant they called the *lousewort*. It is an inelegant name for a plant that deserved better and that we know by the more charming name of *wood betony*.

The wood betony is a spring plant of roadside banks, open woods, clearings, and copses with thick short spiked blossoms that rise above rosettes of coarse hairy fern-like leaves. At first the flowers are greenish-yellow but with added bloom, as the spike increases in length, the arched upper lip becomes a dark purplish-red, the lower lip remains a greenish yellow, and the throat turns red. The stem is rather hairy and is often stained with dull-magenta as are the feather-shaped lower leaves.

The flowers are tubular and two-lipped; the prominent upper lip is dull dark-whitish, opaque magenta, and strongly curved in a hook-shape with a two-toothed tip. The lower lip is three-lobed and dull green-yellow. The light-green calyx is coarse and hairy and tinged at the edge with dull crimson-magenta. There are four stamens located under the hooded upper lip where they are well protected from rain or other pollen destroying agents. Leaf-like bracts are present beneath the flowers. As the flowers develop the flower cluster, which is at first dome shaped, lengthens to an oblong shape. The flowers are fertilized mostly by bees, with the bumblebees and mining bees being the most common visitors. The fruit is a sword-shaped slightly beaked capsule with an opening slit on the upper side.

Thomas Meehan wrote in *Native Flowers and Ferns of the United States,*

> *Common wood betony seeks shade from the warm sun by taking to open woods, or getting on rising knolls in swamps or low grounds where it may have the advantage of a humid atmosphere. The flowers are among the handsomest of our native plants, and the fern-like leaves set off to great advantage the floral beauty.*

And in *A Guide to the Wildflowers* Alice Lounsberry wrote,

> *We have seen in the snapdragon family how many of its members have curious expressive faces, resembling animals quite as much as often pansies take on the look of old men and women. The turtle-heads are like tortoises, the monkey-flower tells its own story, and here, moreover, is the wood betony rearing its slender corolla as the head of a walrus and even with two miniature projections in imitation of his tusks. Most often the upper lip of the flower is purple and the under one pale red, but also they occur in yellow . . . It is ever a strange-looking plant.*

Dutchman's Breeches

The dutchmen wear them

In spite of its rather inelegant name the *Dutchman's breeches* has a certain air of refinement. It is revealed in the finely dissected leaves and dainty heart-shaped blossoms—pendent from the trembling stem as a gem hangs from a lady's ear—which suggests the feminine rather than the masculine.

The Dutchman's breeches is a dainty plant of early spring found in rich rocky woodlands. It has a feathery compound leaf on a long stem that proceeds from the root. This leaf is grayish-green in color and somewhat blue and paler beneath. Its leaflets are finely cut in three parts—that is, they are distributed tri-foliately. Like the leaf petiole, the flower stem also proceeds from the root and usually bears four to eight nodding white flowers that are pantaloon in outline. They consist of two scale-like sepals and four petals that are in two pairs. Two of the petals form a double two spurred somewhat heart-shaped sack. The other two are within the sack and are small, narrow, and united protectively over the slightly protruding stamens. The spurs are tipped with pale yellow.

The tongue of the honeybee is too short to reach the nectar secreted in the two deep spurs. Butterflies have a long enough tongue but it is difficult for them to cling to the pendulous blossoms. Hence cross-fertilization is effected mainly by the early bumblebees.

Wild Geranium

A close relationship

Beginning in April and continuing into July the wild geranium decorates the woodlands, the wooded roadside, and the shady thicket with a purplish bloom that cannot fail to attract our attention. And thereby hangs a tale.

Many years ago Sprengel, the German botanist, had his attention drawn to the close relationship that exists between plants and insects while trying to determine the reason for the hairy corolla of his native geranium. In 1787 he wrote: "the wise author of Nature has not made even a single hair without a definite design." A hundred years or more before, the English botanist, Nehemias Grew, expressed the view that it was necessary for pollen to reach the stigma of a flower in order for it to set fertile seed. Very likely he was the first to observe sex in plants. He also expressed the opinion that a flower is fertilized by insects that carry its pollen from its anthers to the stigma. It was left to Darwin to advance the theory that cross-fertilization—the transfer of pollen from the anther of one flower to the stigma of another—is the end to which all flowers strive. Many clever mechanisms have been developed for that purpose. In short, cross-fertilized flowers are victorious over self-fertilized flowers in the struggle for survival. And perhaps no flower has devised as ingenious a way to prevent self-fertilization as the wild geranium. The pollen becomes mature and the anthers fall away before the stigma has become receptive. Though the flower is perfect the two reproductive structures will not be present at the same time. During cold, rainy, or cloudy weather the flower may retain its anthers for several days before the stigma becomes receptive. On a warm sunny day, when insects are flying, the change may take place within a few hours. The flowers are cross-fertilized mostly by honeybees, the smaller species of mining bees, and the flower-flies. Sometimes the common sulphur butterfly will pilfer a little nectar without performing any service in return.

The wild geranium—also known as the *cranesbill* because of the shape of its fruit—is a plant, one to two feet in height, with a hairy stem, deeply cut gray-green leaves that are five-lobed and covered with rough hair, and magenta-pink or lavender flowers. These occur in loose clusters of between two and five. There are five pointed sepals, five rounded petals, one pistil, and ten stamens. Five of the stamens are longer than the others. The fruit is a slender capsule tipped with a long hooked beak and is known as an explosive fruit. In other words, when the seeds are ripe the capsule opens and discharges them a considerable distance.

In *Happy Hunting-grounds*, William Hamilton Gibson wrote that

> in the cranesbill the mechanism of its seed pod may be likened to the catapult of antiquity, that is the sudden release of a compressed spring. The full powers of this tiny catapult of the cranesbill has never been appreciated . . . but it is only comparatively recently, when walking in the midst of a retreat in the park, that I became fully aware of their energy. It was a still, sultry day in June, which so increased the hygrometric tension of the fast ripening pistils. . . .
> They were quivering right and left. Occasionally a stray missile would strike my face or hand. Altogether the cranesbills were having a time of it; their volleys kept up an incessant bombardment. Curious to investigate the matter further, I picked a large number of the fruiting stems and carried them home for experiment . . . The white cloths spread upon the floor were soon peppered to the distance of ten feet, and observing that many of the seeds fell from a rebound against the end wall and the ceiling, I opened up the passageway and a few hours later here discovered a half-dozen of the black seeds over thirty feet away from their original position. It is hardly improbable that one of them more ambitious than the rest succeeded in reaching the open window and made the jump into my grass plot.

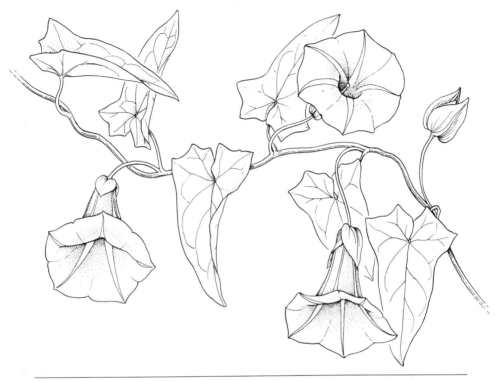

Hedge Bindweed

In suffocating embrace

If we ramble about the countryside during the summer we are most likely to see a vigorous vine with pretty bell-shaped pink and white flowers trailing its way over a stone wall or winding its way about the shrubbery of a wayside thicket. We are reminded of the morning glory of our gardens, and well we should be for they are kin. As a matter of fact, the plant that we just described is often called the *wild morning glory*—though it is usually known as the *hedge bindweed*. That name suggests a somewhat sinister meaning, a kind of evil plant that grips and seizes other plants. And if they are weaker than it is the results may prove disastrous. To be sure the hedge bindweed may at times be a pernicious and obnoxious weed.

Common along fencerows, wayside hedges, and in thickets and fields, the hedge bindweed is a smooth stemmed vine, three to ten feet in height. It has arrow-shaped triangular grayish-green leaves, acute pointed with slender stems, and handsome bell-shaped or funnel-shaped solitary flowers that are about two inches long. The flowers are pinkish with white stripes and borne on long stems. The five stamens are cream-yellow, the pistil is white, and the five-parted calyx is enclosed in two pale-green bracts. The fruit is a globular capsule that may contain four seeds, but usually only two or three are fertile. The seeds are angular, kidney-shaped, and dark-brown.

We usually find the goldbug clinging like a drop of molten gold to the leaves. Few insects have the matchless beauty of this tortoise beetle. The American entomologist, Thaddeus Harris, in writing about it said:

> when living it has the power of changing its hues, at one time appearing only of a dull yellow color, and at other times shining with the splendor of polished brass or gold, tinged sometimes also with variable tints of pearl. The wing-covers, the parts which exhibit a change of color, are lined beneath with an orange colored paint, which seems to be filled with little vessels; and these are probably the source of the changeable brilliancy of the insects.

There are several goldbugs but the species that Harris wrote about is the golden tortoise beetle.

Cattail

Brown red wands on the landscape

Is there anyone who is not acquainted with the cattail, especially in late summer when the picturesque red-brown wands become conspicuous on the landscape? Like other aquatic plants—for example, the reeds and bulrushes—the cattail is admirably suited for living in a watery environment. Its roots are fine and fibrous and especially adjusted to threading the mud of marshy ground. Its leaves are long, thin, and strong and, being flexible, yield to the wind rather than defy it. In June and July the tip of the cylindrical flower stalk will be covered with a fine drooping fringe of olive-yellow that is seen to be a mass of crowded anthers packed with pollen when examined closely with a magnifying glass. This pollen falls below to the pistillate flowers on the same flower stalk or is showered to neighboring flowers with every passing breeze. It is virtually useless to look for the pistillate flowers for, lacking petals and sepals and covered with down, they are hidden from view. Even with the aid of a magnifying glass they are difficult to find. It is the down, of course, that forms the familiar cattail of late summer and early fall. Fluffy hairs attached to the tiny nut-like fruits aid in wind dispersal. They have been used in stuffing pillows and the leaves have been used in the manufacture of matting.

The flower head of the cattail does not appear to be a likely place for an insect to dwell in and yet females of the little cattail moth lay their eggs in the lower pistillate half of the flower spike. When the eggs hatch the caterpillars spin silken threads to form a protective covering that also serves as a snug retreat from the hazards of winter. The silken threads also fasten the seeds in place and thus assure the caterpillars of an adequate food supply until the time comes for them to pupate. As many as 76 cocoons have been taken from a single cattail spike.

Other insects also find the cattail an hospitable food plant. During the summer plant lice suck the juices of the leaves, two species of leaf mining moths tunnel in them, and the larvae of a snout beetle feed on the starchy core of the rootstalk. The Indians also used the rootstalk for food, grinding it into a meal, and it is said that the early settlers of Virginia were fond of the roots. The roots and the lower part of the stem have both been used in salads and it is said that the young fruiting spikes are edible when roasted.

The cattail marsh is the home of the red-winged blackbird and there we can see it perched on a swaying stem, sable plumage shimmering in the golden sunshine, or flashing red as it streaks across the open water. We can listen to its familiar song, which somehow seems to strike an optimistic note in the pervading gloom of the marsh. Indeed, this bird is so inseparable from and so much a part of the marsh that he is not often seen elsewhere. The marsh wren is also a bird of the cattail marsh but it will not often be seen except by those willing to brave the treacherous ooze and swarming mosquitoes. Perhaps the best way is to float silently in a canoe along the marshy shore of a sluggish river.

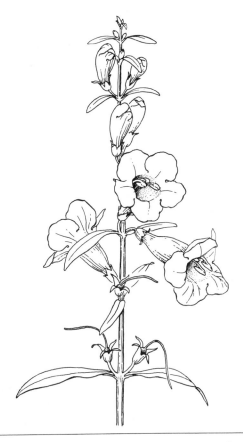

Downy False Foxglove

To perpetuate a memory

John Gerarde, the famous English herbalist, never knew he was to be honored by Linnaeus who gave his name to a group of charming American plants, the genus *Geradia*. He died before the Swedish botanist was born and likely Gerarde never saw any of these plants. Some of them are called *false foxgloves* to distinguish them, probably, from the genus of true foxgloves. The downy false foxglove is one of the former, a handsome plant with a grayish, downy, and erect simple stem and ovate lance-shaped, broad based, slightly coarse and dull toothed yellow-green leaves. The leaves have a wavy edge and are as downy as the stem. The showy pure yellow or light-lemon flowers are about an inch and a half long and trumpet-shaped. The corolla is five lobed with a broad throat that is downy on the inside. The calyx is five-toothed, the four stamens are in pairs, and the flower has a single pistil. These flowers are set in a close terminal cluster that is rather one-sided. The downy false foxglove is two to four feet in height, blossoms from July to August, and occurs in woodlands and thickets. It is cross-fertilized mostly be butterflies and bumblebees and serves as food for the caterpillars of the buckeye or peacock butterfly.

Blue Toadflax

Wearing an air of injured innocence

In her book, *Nature's Garden*, Neltje Blanchan wrote of the blue toadflax: "Sometime lying prostrate in the dust, sometimes erect the linaria's delicate spikes of bloom wear an air of injured innocence; yet the plant, weak as it looks, has managed to spread over three Americas from ocean to ocean." If appearances can be deceiving this is a case in point for this seemingly weak and delicate plant has been hardy enough to spread throughout the country. We now find it blooming from June to September in abandoned fields and generally in open, dry, shady, or rocky places.

It is an extremely slender and smooth species with a few small linear light-green leaves scattered along the stem. These leaves are toothless, stemless, smooth, and shining. The small pale-violet or lavender flowers are about a third of an inch long, two-lipped, and spurred. They have a five-pointed calyx and a two-lipped corolla with the spur curved longer than its tube that is almost closed

217

by a white two ridged projection or palate. The upper lip is erect and two-lobed, the lower spreading and three-lobed. There are four stamens and a single pistil. Unlike its relative, the butter-and-eggs, the blue toadflax has a corolla that is so contracted that bees are unable to reach the nectar. Flies visit the flowers also but it is the butterflies that are especially attracted to the slender spurred flowers and that attend them in the greatest numbers. As these butterflies cannot secure the nectar without touching both the anthers and the stigma they are the chief agents of cross-pollination.

Sundrops

Of floriform sunshine

When a flower of the sundrops opens to advertise its wares to various insects it is as if a burst of sunshine has suddenly penetrated a murky cloudy sky. Sometimes only one flower on a stalk opens at a time, perhaps to increase the possibility of cross-fertilization, but when many open and they are open all day they invite our acquaintance if we are not already familiar with them.

The sundrops blooms from June to August in fields, meadows, road-sides, and waste places. It has a rather slender stem, one to three feet in height, that is usually branched and usually covered with fine hairs though sometimes it is smooth. The stem holds alternate oblong to lance-shaped leaves that are slightly toothed. The flowers are in terminal leafy bracted spikes. They are one-half inch to an inch broad, though sometimes they can be nearly two inches broad, and the petals are notched at the outer end. Their color is a lustrous golden-yellow. The tube of the calyx is much longer than the ovary and its lobes are narrowly lance-shaped and spreading. The stigma extends far beyond the anthers so that self-fertilization is not possible without the aid of insects. The seed pods are about a half an inch long, four angled, and winged. Cross-fertilization is effected primarily by the butterflies and bees but wasps, flowerflies, and beetles also visit the flowers for their abundant pollen.

Pussytoes
With charming rosettes

If we are so inclined we might, on some early spring day, visit a field or rocky pasture and see the pussytoes unfold their little clustered heads; tufts of silver-white silk rise from charming rosettes that can be found throughout the winter. The pussytoes has its staminate and pistillate flowers on separate plants. The staminate flowers have somewhat more color and are dotted in appearance; the pistillate flowers are smooth and covered with soft downy-like "cottony mittens" as one writer put it. Because of its stoloniferous habit it tends to form broad, dense patches. The male and female groups are usually distinct but rather close together—in other words, quite neighborly. The root leaves are obovate to spatulate, three ribbed, and tufted in a small rosette and have soft white wool on both sides. The stem leaves are few, small, and sessile. At first the stems are very short but later they may grow to be six inches or a foot tall. The flower heads occur in small clusters with each head less than a quarter inch broad. The pistillate ones are purplish-brown at the base, with narrow white tips, and have two cleft crimson styles. The staminate ones have broad white petal-like tips. After fruiting, the plant spends the rest of the growing season sending out runners with young plants at the tips. These take root and increase the size of the patches. The mining bees and various flies help in transferring pollen. The hunter's butterfly may also be seen hovering about the flower heads.

Common Violet
and Violets
Of fond remembrance

Anyone who goes botanizing in early spring knows that many of the wildflowers that appear at this time of the year can be found merely by going to the places where they grow—to the woodland swamp for the skunk cabbage, to the pasture for the cinquefoil, or to the hillside thicket for the wood anemone. Others, like the hepatica, the mayflower, and the wild ginger, require a bit of searching. All of these flowers and many others too are firmly fixed in our affections—even the skunk cabbage in spite of its name and unseemly odor. But a perennial favorite of mine is the violet. There are a number of species—80 or so in our country—but whenever the wild violets are mentioned it is the common violet that usually comes to mind. It blossoms everywhere—in the woods, along the roadsides, and in fields, meadows, and marshes. However, it blossoms best in cool shady dells:

> The violet blooms with every spring
> With every spring the breezes blow
> And once again the robins sing
> A song more sweet than June can know.

One thinks of violets as low growing herbaceous plants—as they are in temperate regions—usually found in bunches with flowers peeping out from among the leaves. We are unmindful of the fact that some members of the violet family become shrubs and even small trees in the tropics. Our violets belong to the genus *Viola*—the classical Latin name for the violet. They are low growing plants, generally of tufted habit, with both basal and stem leaves. The basal leaves are simple, heart-shaped or oval, sometimes lobed, stalked, and toothed. The stem leaves are alternate, simple, oval, usually stalked, and toothed also. Two stipules at the base of the stem leaves are usually cut into three lobes. The flowers are stalked, solitary, and sometimes nodding and have a calyx of five sepals and a corolla of five petals. Four of the petals are arranged in pairs, each pair being different. The lower petal is spurred. The flowers also have five stamens and a one-celled ovary with many ovules. The fruit is a three-celled capsule opening elastically.

Unfortunately violets hybridize rather easily so that identifying them becomes a matter for a trained botanist. However a number of them can be readily recognized by their general pattern and, though violets are found in a variety of habitats, most species usually prefer just one kind of situation, which helps to identify them.

The violets are divided into two groups—those having the leaf stalks coming directly from underground rootstalks, the so called *stemless* species, and those having the leaves coming from a common stem, which are known as the *leafy-stemmed violets.* Our *common violet* is a stemless species, as is the rather familiar and attractive *bird's foot violet*, which can readily be identified by its narrowly divided finely cut leaves and by its habit of growing in dry sandy places. The *early blue violet,* the leaves of which are heart-shaped—like those of the common violet but deeply lobed, at times being cut almost as much as the leaves of the bird's foot—is also a stemless species and common in rich woods. The arrow-leaved violet, with its long arrow or halberd-shaped leaves, is another member of the group and is found in moist open meadows and marshes.

If we were to examine a violet flower closely we would find that it has an upper pair of petals, a lateral pair that is narrower than the upper pair, and a broad lower petal that serves as a resting place for the bees and butterflies that come seeking the nectar. The lower petal extends backward to the stem as a spur or sac that contains the nectar and that gives the violet its characteristic shape. Cross-fertilization is effected by various species of bees and butterflies. The smaller mason bees and the mining bees of the *Halictidae* family are the most useful. The larger bumblebees and the butterflies are generally regarded as mere interlopers.

In many species the flowers are sterile and incapable of producing seeds. The seeds are produced by peculiar greenish flowers that are often mistaken for buds or seed vessels. They are located if not actually underground than not far above it among the leaves. These flowers lack petals. They are known as cleisto-gamous flowers and never open. They are fertilized and develop fertile seed without the aid of insects.

We usually think of violets as being blue, purple, or a similar shade, but there are also white and yellow violets. It is believed, as a matter of fact, that violets were originally white, though some botanists believe they were originally yellow. We can observe in the Canada violet, with its white or pale lavender blossoms, a plant in the process of changing from the white ancestral type to the purple—generally regarded as being the highest point in the scale of chromatic evolution. The sprightly *Canada violet,* usually found in hilly woods, is a member of the leafy-stemmed group. A glance at this robust plant and we would suspect that the members of this group are larger plants than the stemless species.

There are several species of white violets, such as the *lance-leaved violet* and the *sweet white violet*—a sweet-scented species with heart-shaped leaves. Both prefer wet meadows, moist woodlands, and the borders of streams and both have purple veins. The veinings presumably serve as guide lines to the nectaries for insect visitors.

The word violet is so synonymous with the colors blue and purple that it seems unbelievable that a violet could be yellow. Yet we have two yellow species—the *downy yellow* and the *yellow round-leaved violet.* The former has an erect, leafy stem covered with fine hairs, the latter a smooth stem. Both may be found in moist thickets or woodlands, though it is not unusual for them to grow in a dry place, especially the round-leaved species. They have pale golden-yellow flowers with veins of madder purple. The veinings serve as pathfinders to the nectaries for the bees that visit them. The common sulphur butterfly is also an occasional visitor.

The most famous and beloved violet of all is the *pansy.* It is the oldest known English garden flower and was well established by the early seventeenth century. In his *Herball,* in his quaint style, Gerarde wrote of the pansy:

> *that the stalks are weake and tender, whereupon grow floures in form a figure like the Violet, and for the most part of the same bigness, of three colours, whereof it took the syrname Tricolor, that is, to say, purple, yellow, and white or blew; by reason of the beauty and bra-verie of which colours they are very pleasing to the eye, for smell they have little or none at all.*

The word *pansy* comes from *pensee,* French for thought or, indirectly, a remembrance. This is well in keeping with the bright, cheerful, and most delightful of all our flowers. With this in mind we bring to a close our rambles along the bypaths of nature in search of the many flowers that give color to the landscape and that offer a bit of cheer and surcease from our daily toil. Perhaps more important, they provide an open sesame to the world of which we are a part but of which we know so little.

Glossary

Accessory organ   An organ not directly involved in the reproductive process.

Achene   A small dry hard one-celled one-seeded indehiscent fruit.

Aggregate fruit   A cluster of fruits developed from the ovaries of a single flower.

Alternate leaves   Arising singly along the stem.

Annual   With a life cycle that is completed in one year.

Anther   The pollen-bearing part of a stamen.

Apetalous   Without petals.

Aquatic   A plant growing in water.

Asymmetrical   Lack of symmetry, lopsided.

Awn   A bristle-like appendage.

Axil   The angle formed by the upper side of a leaf and the stem to which it is attached.

Banner   Uppermost petal in a pea flower.

Basal leaves   Leaves formed at the base of the stem.

Bearded   With long or stiff hairs.

Berry   A thin skinned fleshy fruit with numerous scattered seeds.

Blade   The expanded portion of a leaf.

Bloom   A whitish powdery or waxy covering.

Bract   A modified leaf associated with a flower or an inflorescence.

Bud   An undeveloped shoot or stem. A small axillary or terminal protuberance on the stem of a plant, consisting of rudimentary foliage or floral leaves.

Bulb   A short underground stem.

Calyx   A collective term for the sepals of a flower.

Capsule   A dry dehiscent fruit composed of more than one carpel.

Carnivorous   Eating or living on other animals.

Carpel   A floral organ which bears and encloses ovules. A simple pistil or one member of a compound pistil.

Catkin   A spike inflorescence bearing staminate or pistillate apetalous flowers.

Clasping   A leaf whose base wholly or partly surrounds the stem.

Column   A structure formed by the union of stamens, style, and stigma, as in orchids.

Cleistogamous   Fertilized in the bud without the opening of the flower.

Compound leaf   A leaf divided into smaller leaflets.

Complete flower   A flower that bears sepals, petals, stamens, and pistils.

Corolla   Collectively, the petals of a flower.

Corymb   A simple inflorescence in which the pedicels, growing along the peduncle, are of unequal length with those of the lowest flowers being longest and those of the highest flowers, shortest.

Creeper   A trailing prostrate plant.

Cross-pollination   The transfer of pollen from the stamen of a flower of one plant to the stigma of a flower of another plant.

Cyme   A flower cluster in which the growing apex ceases growth early, all its meristematic tissue being used up in the formation of an apical flower. Other flowers develop farther down on the axis, the youngest flower appearing farthest from the apex.

Deciduous   Plants that regularly lose their leaves each year.

Dehiscent   Splitting or opening along definite seams when mature.

Dioecious   Having the male and female flowers on separate plants.

Disk flower   The small tubular flowers in the central part of a floral head.

Downy   Covered with down or with pubescence or soft hairs.

Dissected leaf   A deeply cut leaf, the cleft not reaching the midrib.

Drupe   A simple fleshy fruit in which the inner wall of the ovary becomes hard and stony and encloses one or two seeds.

Druplet   A diminutive drupe.

Egg   The female germ cell of a plant.

Egg cell   The female germ cell, or egg proper, exclusive of any envelopes derived from or consisting of other cells.

Elliptical   Oblong with rounded ends.

Embryo   The rudimentary plant within the seed.

Emergent   An aquatic plant with its lower part beneath the surface of the water and its upper part above the surface.

Epiphyte   A plant growing on another plant but deriving no nutrients from it.

Evergreen   Having green leaves all year.

Fertilization   The union of a mature sperm cell with a mature egg cell.

Filament   The slender stalk of a stamen that supports the anther.

Flower   The characteristic reproductive structure of flowering plants.

Follicle   A dry fruit developed from a single ovary, producing several or many seeds, and composed of one carpel which splits along one seam.

Fruit   A matured ovary or cluster of matured ovaries.

Gland   A small structure secreting an oil or nectar.

Glandular   Bearing glands.

Head   A dense cluster of sessile or nearly sessile flowers on a short axis or receptacle.

Herb   A plant that does not develop much woody tissue.

Imperfect flower   A flower that bears only stamens or only pistils.

Incomplete flower   A flower that lacks one or more of the four kinds of floral organs.

Indehiscent   A fruit that does not split open along regular seams.

Inferior ovary   Ovary located below sepals, petals, and stamens.

Inflorescence   A flower cluster.

Involucre   A circle or collection of bracts surrounding a flower cluster or a single flower.

Irregular Flower   A flower whose petals are not uniform in shape but are usually grouped to form upper and lower *lips*.

Keel   A ridge like the keel of a boat; in a pea flower the two lowest petals are united to resemble a keel.

Lateral bud   An axillary bud.

Leaf   A lateral green expanded outgrowth of a stem.

Leaf axil   The upper angle between a leaf petiole and the stem from which it grows.

Legume   A simple dry dehiscent fruit formed of a pistil and splitting along two sutures.

Linear   Long, narrow, with parallel sides.

Lip   Each of the upper and lower divisions of a bilabiate corolla or calyx.

Lobed   Indented on the margins.

Meristematic tissue   A tissue whose cells are capable of frequent division and thus are responsible for growth.

Midrib   The central or main rib of a leaf.

Monoecious   Having staminate and pistillate flowers on the same plant.

Multiple fruit   A cluster of matured ovaries produced by several flowers.

Nectar   A sweet liquid produced by flowers.

Nectary   A floral gland that secretes nectar.

Node   The place on a stem where a leaf or a branch is attached.

Opposite leaves   Occurring in pairs at a node, with one leaf on either side of the stem.

Organ   An associated group of tissues for the performance of a particular function.

Ovate   Egg-shaped or having an outline like that of the egg.

Ovary   The basal part of the pistil in which seeds develop.

Ovoid   Egg-shaped.

Ovule   A structure in the ovary of a flower that, when fertilized, can become a seed.

Palate   A rounded projection of the lower lip in two-lipped flowers that closes or nearly closes the throat.

Palmate   Having three or more divisions or lobes that resemble the outspread fingers of a hand.

Panicle   A compound inflorescence that has several main branches with pedicellate flowers arranged along its axis.

Papilionaceous   Having a standard, wings, and keel, as in the peculiar corolla of the sweet pea.

Pappus   Any appendage or tuft of appendages forming a crown of various characters at the summit of the achene.

Parasite   A plant that lives in or on another organism or from which it derives nourishment.

Pedicel   The stalk of an individual flower.

Peduncle   The stalk of a solitary flower, or the main stalk of an inflorescence.

Perfect flower   A flower that bears both stamens and pistils.

Perianth   The floral envelope; the calyx and corolla taken together.

Petal   A floral leaf in the whorl between the stamens and sepals; the basic unit of the corolla.

Petaloid   Petal-like.

Petiole   A leaf stalk.

Pinnate leaf   A compound leaf with leaflets along the sides of a common central stalk.

Pistil   The ovule producing part of a flower, consisting of ovary, style, and stigma.

Pistillate   With pistils only; applied to a flower with a pistil or pistils but no stamens.

Pod   A dry dehiscent fruit splitting along two sutures.

Pollen grain   The male reproductive tissue of flowering plants.

Pollinia   Coherent masses of pollen grains, often with a stalk bearing an adhesive disk.

Pollination   The transfer of pollen from an anther to a stigma.

Pubescence   An epidermal covering of soft short hairs or down.

Raceme   A simple inflorescence in which the flowers, each with is own pedicel, are spaced along a common more or less elongated axis.

Ray flower   The bilaterally symmetrical flowers around the edge of a head.

Receptacle   The enlarged end of the stem to which the parts of a flower are attached.

Rhizome   A horizontal underground stem.

Rosette   A crowded cluster of leaves, usually at the base of the stem, appearing to grow out of the ground.

Runner   A stem that grows on the surface of the ground, often giving rise to new plants at the nodes or tip.

Saprophyte   A plant without chlorophyll and living on dead organic material.

Scale   A rudimentary leaf serving to protect a bud before expansion, such as a bud scale.

Seed   A complete embryo plant protected by one or more seed coats.

Segment   One of the parts of a leaf or other like organ that is cleft or divided.

Self-fertilization or Self-pollination   The transfer of pollen from the stamen to the stigma of the same flower or of another flower on the same plant.

Sepal   The outermost floral organ, usually green, which encloses the other parts of the flower in the bud.

Sessile   Lacking a stalk, attached by the base without a stalk or stem.

Silique   A simple dry dehiscent fruit developed from two fused carpels that separate at maturity, leaving a persistent partition between.

Simple leaf   A leaf with an undivided blade.

Spadix   A spike with a fleshy axis.

Spathe   A large bract or a pair of bracts enclosing an inflorescence.

Sperm cell   The male reproductive unit.

Species   A distinct kind of plant.

Spike   An inflorescence in which the sessile flowers are arranged on a more or less elongated common axis.

Spur   A hollow sac-like or tubular extension of some part of a blossom.

Stamen   The pollen producing organ of a flower.

Staminate   Having stamens only; applied to a flower with stamens but no pistils.

Standard   The upper dilated part of a papilionaceous corolla.

Stem   The main ascending axis of a plant.

Stigma   The part of the pistil, usually the apex, that receives pollen and on which the pollen grains germinate.

Stipule   A small appendage, often leaf-like, on either side of some petioles at the base.

Stolon   A stem growing along or under the ground.

Style   The usually attenuated part of a pistil connecting the ovary and stigma.

Succulent   Fleshy and thick and storing water.

Tendril   A slender twining structure that aids climbing plants.

Toothed   With a saw-like edge.

Tuber   The enlarged fleshy part of an underground stem.

Umbel   An inflorescence in which the stems of the flowers are of approximately the same length and grow from the same point.

Undulate   Having a wavy edge.

Unisexual   A flower of one sex only.

Venation   The arrangement of the veins in a leaf.

Whorl   A circle of three or more leaves, branches, etc. at a node.

Wing   The lateral part of a pea flower.

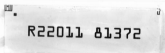